More praise for Congo's Environmental Paradox

'This remarkable, fact-filled study will undoubtedly rank as required reading for anyone with an interest in the DRC   ecialists or for the general reader. Fol   ; should confirm Trefon's standing as   ers and analysts of that central Africa
Edouard Bustin, Boston U

'The first successful attempt to take stock of emerging trends in Congo's natural resource sectors. Well-written, clearly structured and thoroughly documented, Trefon offers fresh analysis on the gap between resource potential and socio-economic development.'
Jeroen Cuvelier, University of Ghent

'A remarkable guide to the tangled relationships between minerals, water and other sectors of the political economy in the Congo. It goes beyond slogans such as "rich land, poor people" to explain how the rich get richer while the poor struggle to survive. Indispensable reading for humanitarians and human rights advocates, both Congolese and international'
Tom Turner, author of *The Congo Wars: Conflict, Myth and Reality*

About the author

Theodore Trefon (PhD, Boston University) studies the politics of state–society relations and natural resource governance in the Democratic Republic of the Congo at the Belgian Royal Museum for Central Africa. He has devoted his career to the Congo as a researcher, author, project manager and consultant. Having lectured on development at the Catholic University of Leuven (KUL) and Boston University Brussels, he continues to teach and learn about environmental governance at Kinshasa's ERAIFT (École Régionale Post-universitaire d'Aménagement et de Gestion Intégrés des Forêts et Territoires Tropicaux). Trefon coordinated European Union-funded forest conservation projects while working at the Free University of Brussels (ULB) from 1994 to 2006. He has advised international development agencies, governments, think tanks, NGOs and private consultancy firms. Contributing editor to the *Review of African Political Economy* and founding director of the Belgian Reference Centre for Expertise on Central Africa, his expertise derives from desk study, analysis, participatory observation and extensive fieldwork. His previous book, *Congo Masquerade: The Political Culture of Aid Inefficiency and Reform Failure* (2011), also appeared in the African Arguments series.

Published by Zed Books and the IAI with the support of the following organizations:

The principal aim of the **International African Institute** is to promote scholarly understanding of Africa, notably its changing societies, cultures and languages. Founded in 1926 and based in London, it supports a range of seminars and publications including the journal *Africa*.
www.internationalafricaninstitute.org

Now more than a hundred years old, the **Royal African Society** today is Britain's leading organization promoting Africa's cause. Through its journal, *African Affairs*, and by organizing meetings, discussions and other activities, the society strengthens links between Africa and Britain and encourages understanding of Africa and its relations with the rest of the world.
www.royalafricansociety.org

The **World Peace Foundation**, founded in 1910, is located at the Fletcher School, Tufts University. The Foundation's mission is to promote innovative research and teaching, believing that these are critical to the challenges of making peace around the world, and should go hand in hand with advocacy and practical engagement with the toughest issues. Its central theme is 'reinventing peace' for the twenty-first century.
www.worldpeacefoundation.org

CONGO'S ENVIRONMENTAL PARADOX

POTENTIAL AND PREDATION IN A LAND OF PLENTY

THEODORE TREFON

ZED

Zed Books

LONDON

In association with
International African Institute
Royal African Society
World Peace Foundation

Dedicated to the ordinary people of the Congo.

Congo's Environmental Paradox: Potential and Predation in a Land of Plenty
was first published in association with the International African Institute,
the Royal African Society and the World Peace Foundation in 2016 by Zed Books Ltd,
The Foundry, 17 Oval Way, London SE11 5RR, UK.

www.zedbooks.co.uk
www.internationalafricaninstitute.org
www.royalafricansociety.org
www.worldpeacefoundation.org

Typeset in Haarlemmer by seagulls.net
Index: ed.emery@thefreeuniversity.net
Cover design: Jonathan Pelham

A catalogue record for this book is available from the British Library.

ISBN 978-1-78360-244-5 hb
ISBN 978-1-78360-243-8 pb
ISBN 978-1-78360-245-2 pdf
ISBN 978-1-78360-246-9 epub
ISBN 978-1-78360-247-6 mobi

CONTENTS

BOXES, TABLES AND FIGURES

ACKNOWLEDGEMENTS

Telling the story of the DRC's natural resources required reading thousands of pages of relevant books and articles, government and international agency reports, NGO releases and a vast quantity of grey literature. This book is largely a synthesis of this documentation – although a synthesis enriched and inspired by frequent assignments in the Congo and interviews with many friends and experts. Although I have used the documentation centre of the contemporary history section of the Royal Museum for Central Africa and other libraries, it is fair to say that a large number of my sources were found on the World Wide Web. A career of research on Congo/Zaire does, however, enable me to distinguish between reliable internet sources and less reliable ones. Dozens of colleagues in Congo, Europe and North America have been extremely generous and forthcoming in emailing me articles, documents and web links as I informed them of this writing endeavour. I mention these details because it appears that this way of working – for better or for worse – will increasingly shape academic research on Africa.* While it cannot replace fieldwork in most disciplines, it is an emerging research approach.

The idea to write *Congo's Environmental Paradox* took shape as I was working on a book chapter commissioned by David Reed of WWF US for his edited volume on global resource scarcity and environmental priorities for American policy makers.**

---

* See Duffield (2014) and Trefon and Cogels (2006) for a discussion on remote methodologies.
** Reed (2015).

I extend thanks to Pierre Englebert of Pomona College who put me in contact with David. The chapter, entitled 'Congo's environmental Catch-22', discussed the political economy of the various environmental sectors developed in the following pages. It was frustrating addressing these vast topics in a single chapter, so I contacted Stephanie Kitchen (International African Institute) and Ken Barlow (Zed Books) to enquire whether a book on the subject could fit into their African Arguments series. They were immediately supportive, and along with Alex de Waal, one of the series' editors, helped me finalise the book proposal.

Each chapter was read by sector experts who made valuable suggestions for revisions and improvements. They checked facts, made sure that my analysis was on track, confirmed that the chapter sub-sections were appropriate, identified gaps and suggested references for further research. Special thanks go to my bilingual friend Patrick Welby (a development practitioner, well acquainted with Congo's governance issues), who read and commented on the entire manuscript, improving both its content and its style. Miles Irving was both creative and pragmatic in helping with the maps. Judith Forshaw was meticulous and professional in copyediting the manuscript. Thanks also to all of the individuals involved in proofreading, page layout, indexing, cover design and other production tasks.

David Booth (Overseas Development Institute) and Professor Niamh Gaynor (Dublin City University) made constructive comments on the introduction. Chapter 2, on the forest sector, was read by Professor Willy Delvingt (Faculté Universitaire de Gembloux), Carlos de Wasseige (Central Africa Forest Observatory) and Filomena Capela Correia (SODEFOR, a commercial logging company). Professor Eric Tollens (Katholieke Universiteit Leuven), Professor Baudouin Michel (ERAIFT and University of Liège) and Jean-Jacques Grodent (SOS Faim) reviewed the following chapter dealing with land and agriculture. Hassan Partow (United Nations Environment Programme), François Misser (Africa energy expert),

Professor Jean-Claude Micha (University of Namur) and Philippe Tréfois and Pierre-Denis Plisnier (both from the Royal Museum for Central Africa) helped me with the fourth chapter on water. Mohamed Laghmouch, also from the Museum, drew a first draft of the map showing Congo's rivers and lakes. Benjamin Augé (French Institute for International Relations), Daniel Balint-Kurti (Global Witness) and François Misser helped with the fifth chapter on oil. Chapter 6, on mining and minerals, benefited from significant involvement by colleagues from the Museum (Thierry De Putter, Max Fernandez-Alonso and Erik Kennes) as well as from Professor Benjamin Rubbers (University of Liège) and Jeroen Cuvelier (University of Ghent).

The Royal Museum for Central Africa pays my salary to carry out interdisciplinary research in and on the Congo. I feel lucky for this opportunity and am grateful to the Museum for its support and respect for academic freedom. My association with ERAIFT (École Régionale Post-universitaire d'Aménagement et de Gestion Intégrés des Forêts et Territoires Tropicaux) in Kinshasa since 2000 has been an eye-opening experience to look at natural resource management through an integrated perspective. Mutambwe Shango and Noël Kabuyaya, friends from the University of Kinshasa, have helped me understand social dynamics in the Congo through enlightening discussions over the years. Amy Shifflette, my harshest critic and most faithful supporter, accompanied me step by step in bringing this book project to fruition. Thank you for your positive energy and unwavering encouragement, Amy. Finally, I hope this book will inspire my children, Lea and Basil, as they make difficult academic and career choices for their futures.

Map of the Democratic Republic of the Congo, showing provinces, major cities and neighbouring countries

Chapter 1

INTRODUCTION: POTENTIAL IN A LAND OF PLENTY

The paradox

This book is about the political economy of natural resources in the Democratic Republic of the Congo (DRC). A land of plenty with the resources the world needs, this immense central African territory is a resource paradise for some but a social and environmental nightmare for others. No other country in Africa, and few countries worldwide, have such an impressive concentration and diversity of natural wealth. Congo has more than 1,100 mineral substances and is home to the world's second-largest tropical rainforest. Endowed with abundant arable land and an enviable balance of rain and sunshine, Congo's farmers could feed well over a billion people – while also providing new sources of sustainable biofuels. As the African continent's population is expected to double to 2 billion people by 2050, its land could be increasingly coveted and put under pressure. More than half of Africa's fish and water resources are located in this troubled nation whose hydroelectric potential could light up the entire continent. Blue gold, green gold, real gold ... and Congo has oil, too.

The DRC is a place of paradox that fascinates and disturbs. It is a rich country of poor people. A host of international monitoring sources constantly reminds us that there is real poverty – notwithstanding the countless anecdotes of legendary Congolese *joie de vivre*. Is the nominally 'Democratic' Republic of the Congo too rich to fail or too rich to rise? Perhaps this country of superlatives is simply too immense to organise. Is it perpetually on the verge of collapse, or, conversely, is its long-overdue rendezvous with prosperity just around the corner? Many development initiatives are launched; few attain their objectives. Despite its potential to be the 'Brazil of Africa', a long history of poor leadership, corruption, external meddling and resource trafficking has contributed to state failure. This in turn has sabotaged the efficient management of natural resource sectors.

International partners have been actively involved in preparing Congo's economic future since Joseph Kabila was parachuted into the presidential palace in January 2001. The World Bank's position – endorsed by other like-minded protagonists such as the United States, Britain, the European Union, Belgium and, increasingly, Germany – is that growth and stability in post-conflict DRC depends on improved – neoliberal – management of the country's outstanding renewable and non-renewable natural resources. Hobbled by unrealistic expectations of the DRC government's capacity to implement good governance policies in its natural resource sectors and overwhelmed by confusing dynamics in a rapidly shifting resource arena, this stance appears to be not entirely wrong. However, it is certainly flawed, because a vicious circle is firmly in place. Poor natural resource management handicaps efforts to rebuild the state, and because the state is weak, it cannot assert authority or sovereignty over its natural capital. This apparently no-win conundrum, which results from internal and external factors, also contributes to the endurance of ongoing security problems in the east. These challenges, which are also part of a long historical process, ostensibly constitute an inescapable environmental Catch-22 situation: there are few clear answers and no consensus on feasible solutions.

As its title indicates, this book is about environmental paradox. And there are many such examples in the Congo today. How is it that a country with abundant water can have so many people who are thirsty? How can so many Congolese literally live in the dark despite huge hydropower capacity? Why is there so much hunger on fertile land? A decade of robust growth driven by the extractive sectors seems to have resulted in little social development. The role of the state is also paradoxical because it is simultaneously perceived as being part of the problem and part of the solution. This book helps clarify these issues.

Opportunities

This state of play could accommodate the view that the DRC is condemned to always be the land of the future. This book, however, takes another stance. Market forces, globalisation, the engagement of emerging economies, the economic activities of resource-dependent ordinary people and elite politics are converging to redefine the use and value of Congo's assets. There are examples of state reform that are redefining the governance of the natural resource sectors. Congo's economy is growing and is increasingly connected to regional economies and global markets. Its natural resources can contribute to development, although what form this may take – and who will benefit – is uncertain.

This book illustrates the changes taking place in Congo's natural resource sectors: change, yes, but not necessarily improvement. The sectors have all evolved significantly over the past few years and will continue to do so in the near future. This relative dynamism results to some extent from developments on the Congolese political and economic landscapes, but far more directly from outside forces. The global demand for oil, minerals and foodstuffs has transformed much of Africa. More commodities are traded today in Mumbai and Shanghai than in New York and London. Western commodities giants such as Glencore, Trafigura and Vitol are forced to design new strategies to compete with Indian and Chinese consortia. Regional agricultural trading centres have sprouted up in Addis Ababa, Lagos, Mombasa and Kigali, providing new opportunities (and risks) for African farming. South Africa is a confirmed player in mineral trading. Climate change mechanisms such as carbon credits were unheard of only a few years ago. Today, their prices are carefully monitored on global financial markets. Megadeals for infrastructure development are in the making. Congo, as elsewhere in Africa, is a vast construction worksite. Although sometimes controversial, hydropower is an international priority. Because of its resources, this vast territory in the heart of Africa will occupy an increasingly significant place in global capitalism through these emerging dynamics and new partnerships. Shifting economic priorities are reshaping Congo's geo-strategic importance. And thanks to a strengthening civil society, ordinary people are aware of these trends.

Congo's Environmental Paradox reframes development perspectives based on these new natural resource dynamics. The chapters and sections on forests, water, farming and artisanal mining show that these resources and activities already sustain tens of millions of Congolese families. Livelihood options and the quest for well-being are often linked to, or dependent on, these resources, which are also the basis for resilient coping strategies. From this perspective, potential is being met, at least in part. Such strategies may not really help people develop, but they certainly help them survive. Resilience here is predicated on a delicate juxtaposition of human needs and expectations, social constraints and opportunities, as well as the resources themselves. This is a process aptly described by Frances Cleaver as natural resource bricolage.[1] Resilience and bricolage are impressive tributes to the will of the people to take charge of their own destinies. However, these forms of agency do not reflect the government's willingness, or its ability, to make sound and just decisions about how to use the country's resources.

While this book is primarily about power over natural resources, it is also about shared responsibilities to manage them – and this has implications for sustainable development. Through radical reforms of the country's management policies and governance practices,

Congo's forests, agricultural land and water resources have the potential to be developed sustainably, but oil and minerals cannot – because, in essence, they are not renewable. A long-term vision of husbanding revenues earned from them today, for the benefit of future generations, does not seem to be on the political agenda.

Congo has been experiencing uninterrupted growth of over 5 per cent per annum since 2003 (except for 2009, the year after the major global economic downturn). Driven mainly by mining and oil exports, growth in 2014 was 8.5 per cent and it is expected to be at least as robust in the coming years. This constitutes the longest period of sustained growth since independence in Congo but it is also part of an Africa-wide phenomenon. The introduction of a value added tax in 2012 contributed to government revenues, as did the improvement in tax collection performance. Tax revenue as a percentage of gross domestic product (GDP) rose to 21 per cent by the end of 2012, up from 5 per cent in 2000.[2] The World Bank's *Doing Business 2015: Going beyond efficiency* identified Congo as one of the ten top performers worldwide with respect to improving business regulation – albeit starting with a rather poor general ranking.[3] The Hilton chain recently announced the opening of a DoubleTree hotel in downtown Kinshasa, indicating the presence of a business clientele. Inflation is under control and the value of the Congolese franc is stable (in part because it is pegged to the US dollar). The national budget, ridiculously low in terms of volume, has been increasing steadily year after year. The recently completed road between Kisangani and Bunia in eastern Congo has had visible development repercussions for the region, contributing to Governor Jean Bamanisa Saïdi's popularity. Cassava leaves harvested in the morning in Bandundu feed Kinshasa families that same evening thanks to highway rehabilitation. There are also examples of local communities taking charge of their own development: Nande traders in Butembo combined their efforts to build and maintain the city's airport. Admittedly insufficient, these illustrations are undeniably harbingers of greater change.

The role of the government, led by Prime Minister Augustin Matata Ponyo Mapon since April 2012, could also be credited with some of the positive economic and political trends. The longstanding perception that Congolese politicians are incompetent, corrupt and useless may need to be revisited. While evidence of corruption certainly does exist (especially in the lucrative arena of public procurement contracts[4]) it is not entirely naïve to suggest that Matata's technocratic government is not all bad or that Congolese politicians are increasingly pragmatic. Three explanations seem plausible. One, Matata needs to deliver some positive financial management results to keep international donors satisfied so that the flow of foreign aid will continue. Two, opposition politicians are increasingly vocal and powerful, and political competition is on the rise.[5] In addition to criticising the president and secretive elite networks of power, they are also putting pressure on the government. This is part of a shift in the Kinshasa political landscape that seems to indicate a recognition of the need to assimilate the concept of political accountability. Civil society activists and diaspora groups reluctantly concede these points, but stress that efforts at improvement are motivated more by the objectives of incumbency and less by the desire to help ordinary people. Three, a cynical view is that reports of strong economic data are simply invented and do not reflect the real situation. There are most likely elements of truth in each of these interpretations.

The government's efforts probably do play a role, but much of the positive economic data results from a favourable international context. Factors include high levels of foreign direct investment (FDI) and official development assistance (ODA). The DRC is the world's largest recipient of ODA.[6] Generally strong commodity prices, a major debt relief package in 2010, the China factor (investment, imports and lending), improved security in most regions and the implementation of a significantly revised regulatory framework (initiated in 2002) are other elements. These factors are fragile and result more from external influences than from meaningful change in domestic policies.[7] They are also representative of Africa-wide trends, especially that of growth resulting from a resource boom.[8] Other than in mining, there is little industrial investment taking place in the DRC today.

This fragility is indicative of another paradox: growth without development. The contrast is striking. Despite apparently strong macroeconomic data, DRC remains in the second-to-last position in the United Nations' Human Development Index: 186 out of the 187 countries ranked.[9] Benefits accrue to the happy few, specifically Congolese elites, their cronies and multinational companies. Nonetheless, this last opinion needs to be carefully nuanced. First, it would not be surprising if the DRC improved its development rankings in the not-too-distant future. In terms of data gathering, analysis and reporting, development indicators may lag behind those for growth. Second, and more importantly, some economic trickle-down is taking place. It may be premature or inaccurate to identify them as a 'middle class', but new social groups and households with discretionary income are emerging.

Indicators include the construction of comfortable new houses and rental properties (people are increasingly confident about acquiring real estate and exercising their property rights in urban areas so are less fearful of whimsical expropriation), an improved and growing fleet of costly motor vehicles, attendance by Congolese children in private schools, considerable expansion in banking and telecommunications services, a visible increase in expensive consumer items, ongoing attention to fashion, attractive shops and supermarkets, the mushrooming of fancy restaurants, international medical travel, rising expectations for leisure and entertainment – and perhaps less stress at the end of the month to make ends meet thanks to slightly higher salaries that are paid on time.

After years of virtual isolation, mobile technology in the form of smartphones, tablets and laptop computers now connects Congolese amongst themselves and to the outside world, with positive ramifications for political debate, networking and business opportunities. Foreign business communities (mainly Lebanese, Indian, Pakistani and Chinese) contribute to these patterns of consumption and change, but it is undeniably a Congolese – mainly urban – phenomenon. A narrowing of the gap between very rich and dirt poor is certainly not taking place rapidly, nor is it comprehensive, but there are hints that this trend is emerging. While there is no way of determining with any precision if it is driven by the natural resource economies, commerce, international aid, diaspora remittances or corruption money, it would be safe to assume that it is a combination of all of these dynamics.

An integrated perspective

The primary ambition of this book is to present up-to-date data and analysis of Congo's main natural resource sectors. *Congo's Environmental Paradox* is essentially empirical and argues, sector by sector, that development and state-building initiatives will not take place in the current context of poor governance. Efforts therefore need to be embedded in locally realistic and appropriate natural resource management perspectives, including in the framework of the stalled decentralisation process.

'Growth without development', the 'paradox of plenty', the 'resource curse', the 'poverty trap' and 'Dutch disease' are all relevant analytical concepts, but ones that I have chosen not to address explicitly. Shelves of volumes have already been written on them, some by the world's most influential development specialists. The way in which the chapters are organised – combining a wide range of environmental facts, analysis and governance challenges – can nevertheless be useful to scholars, civil society activists and analysts who may want to dig deeper into how these important concepts apply to the context of Congolese resources.

An abundant volume of literature also exists on state failure, poor governance, regional conflict, the criminalisation and militarisation of the state, unsuccessful democratisation and security problems. These have been the mainstay of political science research on central Africa over the past 20 years.[10] Inevitable references to these issues also appear in the following chapters but they are not the main focus either. Moreover, lengthy analysis that could help account for how and why the Congolese governance context is the way it is would have been somewhat redundant because I have addressed these issues in previous works.[11] Many people interested in contemporary Congo will be able to readily think of books and authors in the disciplines of political science – and perhaps history and anthropology as well. Few, I am sure, would have comparable name recognition in economics or political economy (especially for work in English), in part because economic data collection vanished with the collapse of the formal economy in the 1980s. Related research then came to an end. The political economy analysis presented here can therefore contribute to redressing this research imbalance.[12]

Part of my motivation for writing this book stems from frustration about mainstream discourse and analysis of Congo's natural resources. Articles, reports from non-governmental organisations (NGOs) and policy documents all suffer from an extreme fragmentation. Whatever information does exist about them tends to be sector specific. The scholarly landscape relating to these resources is covered by vertical silos with few horizontal connections. The urgency in trying to come up with management solutions or policy recommendations also means that these writings usually lack historical depth. This is not intended as a critique of a sector-specific approach because it certainly helps us understand these sectors and resources. My intention here is to emphasise a conceptual gap in resource co-dependency – a gap that helps justify this book from a research perspective. I have also included historical accounts of natural resource management where possible and relevant because the trajectory of Congo's resource exploitation does not exist in an historical vacuum, as aptly pointed out by Bogumil Jewsiewicki.[13] The main focus, however, is the period since

President Joseph Kabila came to power in 2001. Much has evolved in the area of resource use and management since then, despite many patterns of historical and political economy continuity.

This book adopts – and advocates for – an integrated approach in analysing the present and future potential of Congo's natural resources. 'Integrated' (sometimes used synonymously with holistic or systemic) refers here to the interconnectedness of natural resources themselves, combined with governance practices, economic activities and the stakeholders involved. These stakeholders include Congolese officials, farmers and miners, international institutions, Western multinationals, new commercial partners and actors in unofficial trade and trafficking networks. Hanson *et al.* have made a similar plea, calling for a 'coordinated approach to natural resource management in Africa'.[14] The following chapters identify linkages between all of these elements and highlight the lost opportunity costs that result from not pegging development policies to them.

The following examples support my argument about why an integrated approach is necessary. Efforts to improve the sustainable management of Congo's forests focus more often than not on the forest sector *sensu stricto*. This is necessary but not enough. Sustainable use of these forests can be achieved only by looking beyond the sector itself.[15] As a consequence, Chapter 2 points to the inevitable links between forests, water, energy (ranging from cooking charcoal to the mega Inga hydroelectric dam) and agriculture. Agriculture – and mainly slash-and-burn practices – is a major driver of deforestation and thus contributes to global climate change. The underdevelopment of hydroelectric capacity causes deforestation and therefore contributes to climate change. This may seem contrary to the view that overexploitation of resources is the problem, which is a common obsession among activists in post-industrial Western economies. Food insecurity in the DRC clearly stems from production and transportation weaknesses but there are other causes too. Artisanal mining is one example because it has tempted large numbers of farmers to trade their hoes and machetes for picks and shovels.

The section on industrial mining draws attention to DRC's energy deficit, which is a serious obstacle to the creation of added economic value. While the extraction of bulk ore is not particularly energy dependent, its transformation is. This forces many companies to rely on petrol-run generators whose operating costs can be as much as ten times that of the electricity supplied by the state. The Kinshasa government wants the country to export value added products, but processing by the mining companies is not economically profitable with such uncompetitive electricity costs.

Inadequate transportation infrastructure, like the energy deficit, is another cross-cutting problem with negative implications for each of the five sectors analysed. This pertains to difficulties in getting crops from field to market, timber from forest to sawmill or port, or minerals from mine to rail and road networks. The oil sector is not seriously handicapped by transport issues today because production takes place near the Atlantic coast. Nevertheless, a looming logistical problem faces upcoming oil production in eastern Congo: the pipeline question remains unresolved due to national political concerns and regional rivalry. Even water distribution is affected by transport issues. Water is abundant, but clean drinking water is not, partly because of unsafe conduits. These are some of the other connections that are highlighted in an integrated way in the following chapters, again emphasising the need to look beyond the resources themselves.

Readers familiar with the political economy of mining wishing to look beyond that sector will most likely broaden their knowledge about the political economy of oil – and they will therefore be able to make meaningful associations. Water experts could be inspired to think differently about forestry or agriculture issues. These are some of the other advantages found in this collage of natural resource stories.

Congo's Environmental Paradox presents the country's five strategic natural resource sectors chapter by chapter. All of these sectors merit entire books in and of themselves (some such sector studies do exist), but this one has the merit of pulling together this information in a single volume for the first time. It is intended primarily for people interested in the Congo and in African environmental issues, but students wanting to learn about global climate change or hydropower politics, wildlife lovers fascinated by Congo's outstanding biodiversity, food security experts interested in fish farming, NGO campaigners tracking land deals or struggling to end the trade in conflict minerals, companies exploring investment opportunities and donors trying to think creatively about aid delivery strategies, as well as students of development more broadly, should all find some parts of this book conceptually useful and socially pertinent.

Chapter 2

FORESTS OF WEALTH
AND MYSTERY

A cross-cutting priority

Congo's forests matter. Why they matter and to whom, their economic worth and intangible value, their geo-strategic relevance, management challenges and linkages with agriculture and energy are the focus of this chapter. Congo's forests offer tremendous potential while already providing subsistence and well-being to millions of ordinary Congolese – unlike industrial mining or oil resources, which mainly benefit national elites and foreign multinationals. Without them, Congolese people would be even poorer than they are now. The Congolese Poverty Reduction Strategy Paper emphasises the economic contribution of forests for obvious reasons. But these forests are vulnerable too, and their longer-term sustainability is uncertain. The Ministry of the Environment does not have the means to manage this amazing natural heritage and consequently depends to a large extent on international partnerships.

This chapter also argues that forest governance is more of a political challenge than a set of technical issues that need fixing. Congo's forests are arenas riddled with greed, opportunism and mistrust, where competing stakeholders vie for power and control. On the local institutional landscape, forest strategies that are conceptually creative and realistic are currently being designed and tested. Although there are vague strategic frameworks, Congo does not have an official forestry policy. There are countless donor-led programmes, projects and commitments, with an array of activities to achieve expected results. There is, however, no consensual vision of how the sector should be managed in the coming decades or how it could contribute to development. Given a history of external meddling, elite politicking and institutional weakness, is Congo's political, institutional and social environment even remotely conducive to improved forest governance? The same overarching political economy question could also be raised with respect to the other resources studied in this book.

The Congo Basin is home to the world's second-largest contiguous tropical rainforest after Amazonia – and most of it is in the DRC. These forests are essential to local populations for their livelihoods. They matter to the international community for their potential role in combating climate change. The sustainable management of Congo's outstanding forest resources is an urgent national issue and an unresolved global challenge. It could help alleviate the dire poverty of Congo's 70 million people, contribute to macroeconomic development and protect biodiversity. These forests could well be home to the plants, roots or barks that will save lives through new medicines yet to be discovered. But HIV originated there too, as did the Zaire Ebola virus – cause of a horrendous haemorrhagic disease probably carried by fruit bats. Innovative forest management is a cross-cutting priority that affects provincial and national economies, social development, relations with Congo's regional partners and its position in the international community. Authorities in Kinshasa could gain considerable international recognition by appropriating the need to minimise forest loss and degradation – just as they stand to lose credibility by not doing enough. In the run-up to the global conference on climate change in Paris in December 2015, the DRC government requested $21 billion from industrialised countries to help conserve its forests.[1]

Solutions to forest management in Congo lie well beyond what is commonly referred to as 'the forest sector'. Associating agriculture and energy with forest management schemes – in a culturally sensitive way – is a prerequisite for environmental sustainability and poverty reduction. It is impossible to have a viable forestry policy without taking into account agricultural practices. It is unrealistic to design forestry policies without taking needs for fuelwood into account. Forest management is also closely related to infrastructure development, population growth, land tenure, mining, protected area conservation and, above all else, governance.

Competing claims to sovereignty over Congo's forests exacerbate this complex entanglement. Whose forests are they? Whose responsibility is it to manage them? Who should pay for conservation programmes? These questions are hotly debated locally and internationally because economic stakes are high. The debate is also emotional because local populations' relations with forests are embedded in centuries-old historical processes that some stakeholders tend to underestimate.

Most Congolese are directly or indirectly dependent on forests. Subsistence, production and trade, spiritual attachment and cultural identity are the fundamental elements of this dependency. Forests provide rural communities with agricultural land, fish, bushmeat, non-timber forest products and building materials. They are the mystical places where the living and the dead rendezvous in ritual ceremonies, where people make the cosmic link between their ancestors and future generations. Forests are also culturally important for initiation rituals and burials. President Mobutu likened Zaire's forests to Europe's cathedrals in terms of tradition and identity.

Every province has some kind of forest cover, which is called *nzamba* in Lingala and related Bantu languages. Sociologically, the concept of *nzamba* is complex. Its meanings can be contradictory, ranging from prestige to punishment. The popular singer Werrason increased his cachet by adopting the epithet 'King of the Forest' (*Mopao na Nzamba*). But forests are also perceived as backward spaces inhabited by country bumpkins. In colonial times, White masters threatened to send their Black workers back to the forest if they were not pleased with them. *Nakotinda yo na nzamba* was a looming preoccupation, roughly translated as 'If you don't watch out, I'll send you back to the bush.' This highlights the sharp cleavage between perceptions of the attractive modern city and the benighted rural world.

Over many centuries, forest dwellers have contributed to the way in which their environments have evolved. These people are integral elements of their ecosystems. Western fantasy, in part created by Henry Morton Stanley's account of his adventurous trek across the Congo,[2] has produced and perpetrated the myth of the primeval jungle. But as Jan Vansina has convincingly demonstrated, the virgin rainforest – a place without men and women – is as much of a myth as Tarzan.[3] This view, however, is not intended to give any credibility to the 'noble savage' paradigm. On the contrary, many central Africans do not engage in environmentally sustainable practices. They have very pragmatic relations with forests and often perceive them as sources of quickly earned cash: forest resources are free and come from God. *Ventre affamé n'a pas d'oreilles* (it is difficult to reason with someone who is starving) is a commonly heard expression in this context.

People are well aware that certain activities, such as commercial bushmeat hunting, are detrimental to the environment. Yet, when they need money to pay for school fees or buy medicines or a new mobile phone, immediate wants override abstract concerns for the future. The attempt to put an economic price tag on these forests is a controversial and politically sensitive exercise, not only for the numerically dominant Bantu populations but even more so for the Mbuti, Twa and other pygmy hunter-gatherers who live primarily in Congo's dense tropical rainforests. These indigenous peoples, who are highly dependent on the wild products of the rainforest ecosystem, number approximately half a million.[4]

Biodiversity and conservation

Congo's forest ecosystems comprise a fragile mosaic of lowland rainforests throughout the central basin, parts of Bas-Congo,

Maniema and parts of the two Kasaï provinces. There are highland forests along the Albertine Rift in much of North and South Kivu and in parts of Orientale, Maniema and northern Katanga. Dry forests and savannahs extend over the northern fringe of Equateur and Orientale and the southern rims of the two Kasaïs and Katanga, and there are patches in Bandundu and Bas-Congo. These types of land cover over 145 million hectares, which represents 62 per cent of the national territory.[5] Their ecosystems derive from an intricate intermingling of forest and water – and human interaction. More than half of Africa's water resources are in the DRC. This forest–water nexus also has important economic implications. Forest degradation and climate change reduce seasonal river navigability and can lead to decreased output at hydroelectric facilities.

These forest mosaics are full of life, wealth and mystery. Congo is undeniably a biodiversity treasure trove and features on Conservation International's list of 'megadiversity countries' – one of only 17 countries worldwide to do so. There are an estimated 1,000 species of birds and the same number of freshwater fish, 421 types of mammals[6] and 302 reptile species.[7] There are 30 primate species,[8] numerous emblematic animals such as elephants, gorillas and chimpanzees, as well as endemic species such as the 'make love not war' bonobo and the strikingly elegant okapi (or forest giraffe). Although taxonomic inventories are incomplete because of insufficient or outdated research, the available information points to equally impressive numbers of plant species (estimated at 10,000), insects, ants and butterflies.[9]

A good part of this amazing biodiversity is found in Congo's protected areas, which cover 11 per cent of the national territory. Of the 50 different protected areas, the most prized are Virunga, Salonga (Africa's largest and home to the endemic bonobo), Garamba (created in 1938 to protect the white rhinoceros whose populations have since been exterminated – rhino horn is worth more than gold on the Asian black market), Kahuzi-Biéga (also home to gorillas, okapis and bongo antelopes) and Upemba in the

Katangese savannah. Okapi, Luki, Maiko and Epulu are some of the other important parks.

Congo does not have the infrastructure, hotel and transport capacity, a friendly administration or the kind of serene ambiance that eco-tourists require. It does, however, have the wildlife, landscapes, mountains and water attractions that will someday draw wealthy nature lovers in the way that many other African countries are doing: for example, eco-tourism is Tanzania's leading foreign exchange earner.[10] As peace and development come to Congo, so could eco-tourists – another high-potential growth sector.

These protected areas fall under the management jurisdiction of the Congolese Institute for Nature Conservation (ICCN), whose triple mandate is to protect biodiversity, coordinate scientific research and promote eco-tourism. UNESCO supports ICCN in the management of Congo's World Heritage sites. ICCN, however, like so many other governmental agencies, is unable to do much. Despite its long history (it was created in 1934), its culture of conservation and committed staff, the challenges it faces are overwhelming. They stem from both within the institute and from outside factors.[11] None of the parks has officially adopted the management plans needed to reach expected conservation objectives.[12] Protected areas have encountered difficulties with local populations, just as logging concessions have. Lack of trust, broken promises, diverging perceptions and mutual disdain are some of the recurring problems. Management approaches tend to be top-down and do not take into account the needs and expectations of local populations.[13] This is a serious issue because conservation cannot take place without respect for local people's social development and improved well-being. Outdated human resource management systems and financial constraints also hamper ICCN's efficiency.

Conservation is also threatened by commercial poaching, illegal fishing, artisanal mining and habitat loss resulting from agricultural expansion. Oil exploitation in Virunga is a looming menace. The presence of armed groups is an ongoing conservation setback and a human tragedy. The deadly Lord's Resistance Army has been active in Garamba, as was the Sudanese People's Liberation Army. Virunga has been threatened by multiple armed forces, including the M23 rebel group, the Democratic Forces for the Liberation of Rwanda (FDLR) and other Mayi-Mayi militia. In recent years, 140 Virunga rangers have been killed protecting the park and civilians. Head warden Emmanuel de Merode was shot in an ambush in April 2014. That morning, he had met with a public prosecutor in the North Kivu provincial capital Goma to lodge a complaint against Britain's SOCO oil company, which is exploring for oil in the park. At the Epulu reserve, militia chief Morgan and his men stormed the main station with AK47 assault rifles in June 2012, killing seven people and all but one of the 16 okapis.[14] These events testify to Congo's legacy of armed conflict that continues to traumatise people and threaten wildlife. Even when armed conflict ends, negative impacts on the environment persist.

This situation of extreme violence also testifies to the urgency needed to find appropriate conservation solutions. Conservation, like other post-conflict state-building priorities, has been carried out by Congo's international partners. Until a generation ago, their actions were largely driven by utopian visions of a threatened Garden of Eden.[15] Today, they are motivated by the more pragmatic opinion that their policies are far from perfect but something has to be done. The European Commission and the United States Agency for International Development (USAID) have been involved in many regional and national conservation initiatives, ranging from strict conservation programmes to research and capacity building. Some notable regional initiatives are Ecosystèmes Forestiers en Afrique Centrale (ECOFAC), Réseau des Aires Protégées d'Afrique Centrale (RAPAC), Congo Basin Forest Partnership (CBFP), the Central Africa Regional Program for the Environment (CARPE) and the convergence plan of the Council of Ministers in charge of the Forests of Central Africa (Commission des Forêts d'Afrique Centrale or COMIFAC). Donors and the public recognise the expertise of international conservation non-governmental organisations (NGOs) and provide them with badly needed funding. Some of the key actors are the World Wide Fund for Nature (WWF), Conservation International, Frankfurt Zoological Society, Max Planck Institute, World Conservation Society, African Parks, Bonobo Conservation Initiative, Dian Fossey Gorilla Fund International and African Wildlife Foundation.

The Tayna Nature Reserve in North Kivu, supported by Walt Disney, is an innovative community-based conservation programme set up by local people according to customary governance practices. In another example, the Howard G. Buffett Foundation has committed $19.7 million to develop a controversial hydroelectric power project in Virunga.[16] This makes sense for some because the park – and the gorilla habitat – is being destroyed to satisfy Goma's need for charcoal. For others, the billionaire philanthropist's projects do not adequately address the needs of local populations who oppose park management policies. WWF has worked closely with people in and around the Luki Biosphere Reserve in Bas-Congo to design alternative livelihood strategies and around Virunga national park to promote the establishment of smallholdings to produce timber on a commercial basis, either for construction purposes or for fuelwood. Another initiative relating to Virunga is an ambitious €14 million project funded by the Global Climate Change Alliance[17] – from the EU – to train a variety of stakeholders at Kisangani University and to promote tree plantations in North Kivu to produce charcoal (locally called *makala*). This is being implemented by the Centre for International Forestry Research (CIFOR). Community forestry, although slow to take shape in the DRC, has gradually been adopted elsewhere in the region. Although still immature in terms of real community management, the trend deserves continued international support. There are, therefore, some emerging achievements in terms of understanding the complexities of biodiversity dynamics, popular awareness, stakeholder partnerships, funding and the promotion of Congo's conservation heritage.

Nuancing the causes of deforestation and degradation

Congo's rich tropical forest heritage is under threat. According to what is probably the best scientific data available (based mainly on diachronic remote-sensing techniques), 'the evolution of gross deforestation between 1990–2000 and 2000–2005 is quite significant'.[18] Between 1990 and 2000, net deforestation in the DRC was higher than in all other Congo Basin countries, and for the 2000–2005 period it was still significantly higher than regional rates.[19] Zhou *et al.*, also using remote-sensing databases, have observed a 'widespread decline of Congo rainforest greenness in the past decade'.[20] Pressure is constant and has a strong cumulative effect. The evidence also shows that national aggregate figures are not particularly meaningful because deforestation and degradation are highly fragmented processes. They take place in forest areas close to urban settlements and roads and in other high population density areas.[21] In the central basin, where population density is low, there is little deforestation. Congo's population is predicted to more than double by 2050 – up from 70 million (2015 estimate) to 148.5 million in 2050. The cultural pressure to have large families is strong and family planning options are largely unavailable in Congo, and particularly so in rural areas. In aggregate terms, therefore, while the vast expanse of Congo's dense tropical forest may not be an environmental hotspot today, some pockets already are, and others are likely to become so in the medium term.

What drives deforestation throughout the Congo Basin and in the DRC in particular? There are multiple causes and they can be grouped into two categories. The widely cited work of Geist and Lambin indicates 'proximate causes', meaning specific human activities (agricultural practices, the development of roads and the cutting down of trees) and social processes (demographic pressure, urbanisation, trade, governance and culture).[22] All of these causes and processes are interconnected. Slash-and-burn agriculture in high population density areas near roads or rivers is the principal driver of deforestation and degradation in Congo (see Chapter 3). Urbanisation is another main driver because urban populations encroach on forests for new housing settlements, agricultural land and wood extraction for fuelwood and building materials. In some instances, however, research shows that 'more people does not necessarily mean less forest', an argument made for areas in West Africa by Fairhead and Leach.[23]

Charcoal

After agriculture, urban needs for charcoal constitute the next most significant cause of forest loss and degradation. City dwellers throughout the Congo have a vital dependence on charcoal for cooking. Fuelwood and *makala* supply at least 85 per cent of all domestic energy needs in Congo. Dependency on *makala* is yet another of Congo's environmental paradoxes because the country has tremendous hydroelectric capacity. The Inga hydroelectric complex, for example, produces an insignificant amount of its energy potential. Rwanda is currently extracting methane gas from Lake Kivu while Congo is not, much to the chagrin of Goma's residents. In addition to mothers who need to cook for their families, activities such as brick making (for house construction), bakeries, restaurants and artisanal alcohol distillers are also big *makala* users.

In some cases, the wood used to make *makala* is a by-product of land cleared for agriculture, but most trees are cut down specifically for charcoal production. As people have no energy alternatives, charcoal production is turning peri-urban space into devastated biodiversity vacuums. The economic and social costs are high, too, because livelihood strategies are disrupted.[24] Well-organised trade networks have developed to make the link between producers (often young urban unemployed men) and consumers.[25] From an employment perspective, the charcoal sector is significant; Schure *et al.* estimate that 300,000 people are involved in the Kinshasa market alone.[26] Assuming that this can be doubled for the national figure – and this is a conservative estimate given the number of large cities – there would be more people involved in the charcoal sector than in the country's entire civil service. This figure also compares with 15,000 workers in the formal logging sector.[27] The business of *makala* demonstrates how people seize opportunities in the fend-for-yourself informal economy, turning constraints into a survival tactic. It reveals how people adapt to situations when public services are inadequate. Profits, however, are relatively modest: most charcoal producers earn less than $50 a month.[28]

Supply depends on the type of forest and the size of the city. Abundant forest resources around Kisangani, for example, mean that the charcoal market is supplied from trees within a relatively close 37-kilometre perimeter.[29] Production takes place between 20 and 30 kilometres from Lubumbashi, from where bags are transported by bicycle.[30] A barefoot man pushing a bicycle laden with up to 200 kilogrammes of charcoal is not an uncommon sight in the urban hinterland. The means of transportation is an indicator of resource availability or scarcity. Kinshasa exerts pressure on forests well beyond its immediate hinterland; cars, pick-ups and lorries transport bags of charcoal from as far as 500 kilometres away in Bas-Congo. Bandundu also supplies Kinshasa via road and river, while some charcoal comes from the distant Equateur province by barge along the Congo River. Tree harvesting is also affecting protected areas such as the Kisantu Botanical Garden, the Luki Biosphere Reserve and the prestigious Virunga National Park, where militias have taken control of the profitable *makala* network to supply the city of Goma as well as Rwanda. Scarcity and the need for cash have put pressure on even valuable fruit trees. Villagers in the Boma hinterland sell mango trees to brick makers who devour huge quantities of wood to bake bricks for the expanding housing market.

There is a multitude of stages and actors involved in the *makala* commodity chain. Entry costs are low (tools are only rudimentary) and no particular technical *savoir faire* is required. For the production phase alone, the steps include negotiating access to a forest with a village chief, felling the trees and cutting them up into the right size chunks, then stacking and blanketing them with earth. Igniting this pile of earth-covered wood (called an 'oven') and then monitoring the carbonisation process can take up to a couple of weeks. The oven is then dismantled and the charcoal is bagged once cool. The complicated process of getting it to consumers follows; again, this involves every imaginable type of transporter, intermediary and governmental parasite.

Given economic hard times, a tendency towards micro-retail is developing. As few families have the wherewithal to purchase an entire bag of *makala*, it is sold in neighbourhood markets in very small quantities – even as little as a single cooking portion. Despite the difficult access to this vital commodity and public awareness campaigns, Congolese women have been reluctant to use the improved cooking stove that has met with so much success in West Africa, opting instead for their old-fashioned *braseros*. For dishes such as beans or cassava leaves, even when electricity is available, they prefer cooking with *makala*. Even those relatively few households with access to electricity or gas invariably have a supply of *makala* in case of power cuts (*délestage*), which occur regularly. Despite official discourse about reinforcing domestic energy supply, the government is not doing much with regard to this social and economic priority. This absence of vision and initiative, combined with a strong cultural attachment to *makala*, means that pressure will continue to be put on Congo's peri-urban hinterlands.

Logging

Congolese are sensitive to the fact that it takes only a couple of hours for a man with a chainsaw to level a tree that has been growing in the forest for hundreds of years. The Congolese government and most international partners officially and publicly concur that the forest is worth far more standing than cut down. But forestry, like mining, is a high-stakes business that pushes unprincipled actors to make deals with corrupt officials. This deal making consists of a barter process whereby rules, codes, costs and practical norms are constantly renegotiated. Certain well-respected environmental NGOs, such as Rainforest Foundation, Greenpeace and Global Witness, have campaigned against industrial logging and the 'rapacious nature of some of the timber operators'.[31] Much of the NGO campaigning, particularly after the 2002 Forest Code took effect, focused on the potentially negative social consequences in and around logging concessions. Some of their arguments pertain to local populations' exclusion from their forests and the links between logging and the opening up of new agricultural areas. Industrial logging also contributes to commercial bushmeat hunting.[32] Even though the social and environmental impacts of artisanal harvesting far outstrip those of industrial logging, they have received significantly less NGO attention, probably because the actors involved are more difficult to identify.

The social cost of industrial logging is high because local populations rarely derive any significant benefits from it – neither in terms of employment nor in terms of revenues. The requirements to build schools and provide healthcare in and around the concessions are respected only half-heartedly at best. Loggers, however, do not bear the sole responsibility: people living in forest areas under concession are not always responsible partners and often have unrealistic expectations concerning socioeconomic investments. While some loggers try to get away with minimum social invest- ments, certain communities expect universities, airstrips and even canals in compensation for logging on what they perceive as their land. These communities, which are generally in need of basic socioeconomic investments, are often unable to decide, in a participatory way, on priorities to present to management teams working with loggers. This also explains why relations between local communities and logging companies tend to be antagonistic. The cleavages, tensions and problems of distrust, as well as gender and generation gaps within forest communities, can be exacerbated by the activities of logging companies.[33]

The Forest Code and the October 2005 presidential decree lay the legal foundations for sustainable, socially and environmentally responsible management. They include substantial requirements for public consultation and integration of social and environmental factors into the forest concession allocation process. In theory, this represents a significant improvement on past laws and practices. One advantage is the way that the new legal framework narrows the gap between customary and modern law. However, in practice, in addition to not providing real benefits to local populations or contributing to macroeconomic growth, the probably too-ambitious terms of the Code are squeezing out of the sector those loggers who pay taxes or try to respect social clauses. The German Danzer group, formerly one of the big actors on Congo's industrial logging landscape, shut down its DRC operations in 2013 for this reason. Greenpeace investigations have identified instances when industrial loggers, taking advantage of regulatory loopholes and inconsistencies, have carried out 'artisanal' logging because it is more profitable.[34] Moreover, the Code contradicts the 2006 Constitution concerning fiscal rights and responsibilities of the central government and the provinces.

From an environmental perspective, research reveals that 'DRC's forest resources are not threatened by industrial operations as currently practiced'.[35] Industrial loggers remove only a few trees per hectare. Because of expensive transport costs and market constraints, they concentrate only on high-value timber. For the time being, Congo's neighbours (Cameroon, Republic of Congo and Gabon) offer more profitable conditions. A perverse argument could be made here that conflict, state failure and infrastructure decline contributed to the preservation of Congo's valuable industrial hardwoods.

Industrial logging is a competitive business that requires meticulous planning and significant financial investment and patience before profits are generated. Factors such as legal access to concessions, the social context and relations with local communities, transportation costs, the availability of skilled workers, the fiscal and legal framework, the possibility of administrative hassles, political security and investment security all have to be carefully considered before venturing into the sector. These are real handicaps in the Congo today and explain why only around ten companies are currently engaged in industrial harvesting. In the past few years, these companies have been harvesting an estimated 300,000 cubic metres of timber annually, the three main tree species being *sapelli*, *wenge* and *afromosia*.

Harvested wood is primarily destined for the European market and is exported as unprocessed timber (around 50 per cent) and partially processed planks, parquets and plywood (making up the other 50 per cent). The industrial logging sector consequently contributes a mere 1 per cent to the national economy – or six times less than in Cameroon.[36] Part of the problem here is the state's inability to collect taxes and, if they are collected, its unwillingness to transfer the money into the appropriate government channels – not necessarily the absence of taxable revenues themselves. Tax legislation and regulations are inadequate and ambiguous, and poor coordination by different collection agencies makes tax collection difficult.[37] Payment methods that are not transparent have prevented reliable disclosure of real tax amounts. Industrial logging's contribution to formal sector employment is also insignificant.

Driven by the needs of growing urban populations, the export market is dwarfed by timber sales on local markets.[38] Informal artisanal harvesting, again in recent years, is estimated at 5 million cubic metres and is destined in large part to house construction and furniture making. Some of Congo's artisanal harvesting is exported to Angola, Zambia, Uganda, Kenya and other East African markets.[39] Artisanal harvesting is commonly referred to as 'informal' or 'uncontrolled' because 'its economic, ecological and social impacts are unbeknownst to the national ministries and unaccounted for in national and international statistics'.[40] The Congolese Association of Small-Scale Loggers estimates that around 8,000 people are involved.[41]

Like many other informal activities in the DRC, such as artisanal mining, artisanal harvesting can be extremely well organised, mainly in terms of equipment (portable mechanised sawmills and chainsaws), access to the trees through negotiations with local chiefs, pay-offs to state agents, and trade and transportation networks. It also takes the form of pit sawing, which is done by a small team of mavericks with a chainsaw or handsaw who carry the planks out of the forest on their heads or by bicycle. Contractors who place orders for specific products sometimes provide chainsaws to local harvesters. Holders of legal concessions complain that these activities also take place in 'their' forests, which constitutes another obstacle to profitability in the formal sector. Although artisanal harvesting is an important source of cash for the workers themselves, the government derives no benefit and considers it illegal. This is another example of the incapacity – or unwillingness – of provincial agencies and the central government to adopt appropriate legislation and to implement controls.[42]

Illegal timber harvesting and trade constitute an environmental threat with global security repercussions because they are 'linked to armed conflicts and exploitation and can indirectly contribute to the occurrence of other crimes such as trade in endangered species, corruption, money laundering and organised crime'.[43] A panel of experts investigating the illegal exploitation of natural resources in the DRC has highlighted these problems in various reports.[44] A 'post-conflict rush for resources'[45] took place in Congo and continues today for timber, animal trophies (mainly ivory and rhinoceros horn) and minerals. The resources themselves are different but the illegal trade patterns are similar.

This kind of trafficking prompted President George W. Bush to sign the Presidential Initiative Against Illegal Logging Act[46] and the European Commission to set up FLEGT (Forest Law Enforcement, Governance and Trade).[47] These initiatives provide a number of measures to exclude illegal timber from US and European markets, to improve the supply of legal timber and to increase the demand for sustainably harvested wood products. They work with other control mechanisms such as the Forest Stewardship Council (FSC).[48] Laudable indeed, but corruption hampers these initiatives. They are also weakened by limited jurisdiction because importing countries (India and China, for example) are neither morally inclined nor legally bound to respect their principles. These counties are increasingly under pressure, however, from European and American consumer groups. This pressure is important because much of the raw timber China imports is exported as finished products.

The British NGO Resource Extraction Monitoring has set up an independent monitoring programme to help Congolese authorities tackle challenges to forest governance.[49] One of their main accomplishments is stimulating local and international awareness about sustainable timber harvesting and the need for far greater transparency in supply chains, resulting in some positive reactions from consumers. Middle-class consumers want to know where the timber for their lawn chairs and construction lumber comes from. Huge retailers such as Sweden's IKEA use only certified timber and Home Depot gives preferential treatment to FSC-certified products.

The legal and institutional context

Serendipity is not going to save Congo's forests. Policies could help but, for the time being, they appear to be off target. The urgency of crisis management has clouded the need for creative policy design and implementation. 'Implement in haste, repent at leisure' is the way one group of critical forest activists has described this problem.[50] The social, economic and environmental dynamics affecting Congo's rich forest heritage take place in a context of poor governance and weak institutions. Legal instruments are relatively new and still immature. Revisions and improvements are still needed, and these require difficult political decisions to be made. Efforts to reduce forest degradation will not be effective until the sensitive issues of land tenure and resource rights, for example, are resolved.[51]

Since the 1992 Rio Earth Summit, it has been accepted that people need to be consulted, informed and involved when elaborating and implementing forest governance policies. While the government and international partners have accepted the principles of consultation and participation, the conceptual and financial means for putting these principles into practice are inadequate. These challenges, in addition to Congo's priceless biodiversity assets, explain why so many foreign actors have invested in trying to establish some order in the sector's management. The Environment Ministry (officially the Ministry of Environment, Nature Conservation and Sustainable Development) relies extensively on international advice and outside funding. The protected area network is run largely by international environmental NGOs with multilateral and bilateral support. The World Bank took a proactive role in the preparation of the 2002 Forest Code.

The Environment Ministry has the triple mandate of sustainably managing the environment, preserving biodiversity and promoting tourism. It has all the appropriate services, departments and work units required to carry out this mission. Most of them, however, exist more on a fictitious organisational chart than in reality. It could be tempting to suggest that the environment in general and forests in particular are not political priorities. The problem, however, is not so simple. The different natural resource sectors are subject to high-stakes wrangling, negotiations and trade-offs between Congolese elites themselves (based on economic interests and regional affinities) and between these elites and international partners. Unlike the Ministry of Mines, the Environment Ministry has simply not been successful in convincing the president and his close associates that the environment is a priority. The interests of powerful elites govern environmental politics in the Congo, and forests cannot compete with far more powerful mining interests. Indeed, patrimonial politics work best when the pay-offs are high. In addition, strategies proposed to improve forest governance require a long-term approach but many Congolese elites think in terms of short-term objectives.

The way in which budgets are established and implemented is proof of this political reality. International Monetary Fund experts are heavily engaged in establishing the national budget, which is a strong testimony about Congo's limited sovereignty. The Environment Ministry has received approximately $37 million per year over the past few years.[52] Disbursements, however, are far lower because they require approval by the Ministers of Finance and the Budget and then have to be paid out by the Central Bank. The sums actually disbursed amount to less than 15 per cent of those budgeted. Payments do not conform to agreed budgets because there is a perception among top decision makers that the donor community is sufficiently generous to the Environment Ministry. In their view, if outside partners pay, there is less need to devote funds from the national treasury. International donor commitments come to between $50 million and $60 million per year, while payments are approximately 80 per cent of those amounts. As more than 90 per cent of all expenditures are devoted to salaries, there is practically no money available for operational expenses, the purchase of office equipment and supplies, travel or investment.

Although it could be assumed that outside funding is appreciated and put to good use, that assumption is flawed. Most of it benefits programmes and projects designed by donors without sufficient consultation with Environment Ministry staff. As with many other donor-driven development initiatives, this is a major cause of frustration and a constant constraint to ownership. In 2004, I visited Eulalie Bashige, the then ICCN director, in her office in Kinshasa. She was seated at a small table in a corner. An adviser from the German Technical Cooperation (GTZ) was sitting comfortably at a large desk in the centre of the office.

Congo has not adopted a national land use plan. This absence of an integrated approach is a constraint to improved management of forest space and resources, as various experts have pointed out.[53] The ambition of drafting a forest land use plan (*plan de zonage forestier*) that could identify land for commercial forestry, rural development, agriculture and conservation has not been achieved. The Environment Ministry alone is unable to cope with peripheral institutional influences. Activities regulated by others ministries (Mining, Land Tenure, Agriculture, Oil and Labour) reveal the inconsistencies and contradictions in national policies. According to the rather serious briefing note from Resource Extraction Monitoring,[54] the level of coordination between institutions responsible for forests is 'inexistent' or 'weak at best'. The most flagrant example of inconsistency is the overlap between mining concessions and protected areas. Javelle and Veit estimate this overlap to be 3.5 million hectares.[55] This estimate, however, is based on dubious official concession data, and, as it does not include artisanal mining, the figure is considerably higher. This is another indicator of how difficult it is to manage the network of protected areas that some concerned ICCN staff and international environmental NGOs are struggling to conserve. Diverging perceptions between customary land use institutions and the inter-ministerial fragmentation of modern law constitute an additional level of complexity.

Despite years of stakeholder participation discourse and internationally financed capacity-building initiatives, Congo has been unsuccessful in narrowing the gap between top-down, centralised policies and the everyday activities carried out by forest-dependent peoples. One potentially important set of stakeholders that has been powerless to act positively in the forest sector is Congolese parliamentarians. They established an Environment and Natural Resource Commission in June 2012, which has approximately 70 members. Although forestry issues are one of its stated priorities, the Commission meets rarely. As both opposition and majority MPs sit on it, internecine wrangling has undermined its potential.[56] This is not surprising because the executive dominates politics – although there is some evidence that this situation is evolving. While relations between the executive and parliament are clearly defined in the Constitution (mainly in Chapter 2, Articles

100–148), the law is generally circumvented. Parliament is supposed to be the main actor in drafting laws but this responsibility has been largely taken over by the government via technocratic experts in the relevant ministries (often with external advice). This institutional context has a direct impact on forest management because social accountability remains a vague concept and policies do not seem to correspond to local realities. In 2012, I carried out interviews with a series of experts about the capacity of Congolese MPs to contribute to environmental management. Responses highlighted the inefficiency of parliament in this domain.

Box 2.1 Parliament's role in forest governance

There are few environmental champions to be found in the Congolese Parliament. UN agencies focus their efforts on ministerial technical staff because they are more effcient than MPs.
    < Expert, United Nations Environment Programme >

MPs are necessary partners on environmental issues … we engage with them partly out of hope … in practical terms there are no real results.
    < Environmental campaigner, Global Witness >

Some parliamentary commissions are very 'juicy' but those relating to forest governance are not.
    < Researcher, University of Liège >

Imagining that MPs in Kinshasa can help improve forest governance is a donor-driven fantasy. People interact with provincial MPs only to ensure that they have access to forest resources for their own survival and commerce, certainly not for conservation.
    < Congolese university professor >

Congolese civil society actors have been only slightly more efficient than MPs. Environmental civil society is developing in Congo, but rather slowly. A few environmental NGOs exist and carry out important awareness, watchdog and conservation work.[57] A good example of this type of work is the pressure that they have been putting on foreign oil companies exploring for oil in the Virunga National Park. But civil society in Congo in general and environmental civil society in particular remains fragile and largely powerless. It does not have the necessary popular support, financial means or professionalism to play the role of a vibrant political force able to combat vested interests. There are no outstanding Congolese civil society champions working on forest governance. And civil society has been infiltrated by government officials, which makes Congo a country with 'governmental non-governmental organisations'. Another problem is the relative artificialness of Congolese civil society. It is boosted financially, conceptually and ideologically by international NGOs. This support makes it difficult to establish how embedded Congolese organisations really are in local communities and how these communities appropriate their message and work.

A number of regional initiatives aimed at improving forest governance exist. CBFP is a voluntary multi-stakeholder initiative with over 40 partners. Donor agencies, international organisations, NGOs, scientific institutions and representatives from the private sector have joined forces to consolidate their capacities to support COMIFAC. Their objective is to promote the conservation and sustainable management of the Congo Basin's forest ecosystems. The Congo Basin Forest Fund (CBFF), launched in 2008, provides accessible funding and is designed to: 1) support innovative proposals that will develop the capacity of the people and institutions of the Congo Basin to enable them to manage their forests; 2) help local communities find livelihoods that are consistent with the conservation of forests; and 3) reduce the rate of deforestation. CBFF received an initial grant of £100 million from the British and

Norwegian governments, but the absence of local-level absorption capacity has slowed down the disbursement calendar. This flurry of well-intentioned commitments, partnerships and funding has provided visibility and has stimulated interest but has not succeeded in significantly improving forest governance in the DRC.

New environmental services

Human activity contributes to global climate change. Even those countries that were reluctant to accept scientific evidence for political reasons (the United States, for example) now recognise that it is a grave threat to our planet.[58] When the Nobel Foundation awarded its Peace Prize to the Intergovernmental Panel on Climate Change (IPCC) in 2013, a clear message was sent. This coincided with a growing international consensus that coordinated action worldwide is urgent. Even erstwhile climate change sceptics are revising their views. The IPCC argues that at least 17 per cent of global greenhouse gas emissions result from deforestation. This is more than all the emissions of the world's transportation sector. Deforestation in the tropics contributes to a significant share of this 17 per cent. Forest governance is therefore one of the priorities of the United Nations Framework Convention on Climate Change. Echoing the findings of the influential Stern review,[59] a high-level group of American policy makers claims that 'without conserving tropical forests it will be virtually impossible for the world to avoid unacceptable risks of dangerous climate change'.[60] This is the case because tropical forests are important reservoirs of carbon – or carbon sinks. This is further proof that global issues and the Congolese environment are intertwined.

Payment for Environmental Services (PES), sometimes called Payment for Ecosystem Services, is a climate change reduction strategy increasingly advocated by some policy makers. PES are voluntary transactions between providers of ecosystem services and users or beneficiaries of those services.[61] Biodiversity conservation, carbon sequestration, watershed protection and forest landscape beauty are considered to be the services with the most market-based potential. Private forest conservation areas are becoming common but account for no more than a few per cent of total protected areas, except in a few southern African and Central American countries. These services differ from the more traditional concept of forest products such as timber and are more difficult to quantify in terms of monetary value. The market has greater difficulty is putting a price on the aesthetics of a waterfall than on a cubic metre of *afromosia.*

It was primarily philanthropists who were concerned by these strategies until recently. Today, profit-seeking investors are also showing interest in them. They are defining conservation finance mechanisms whereby financial investments in ecosystem resources are made to conserve the value of ecosystems for the long term.[62] Advocates of these strategies emphasise that they could be sustainable because they are based on the self-interest of users and providers – not on trends or on the whims of donors and NGOs. Sceptics, however, have valid reasons to be cautious about them. Conservation needs far surpass the global willingness to pay for conservation. The rights of local populations could be deliberately violated to protect vested interests[63] or threatened because agreements and policies are not enforceable.[64] Questions about the reliability of scientific data are also unresolved. How much carbon does a forest really stock, for example?[65] Poor governance, once again, comes to the fore in discussions about PES in central Africa because economic instruments do not work in the absence of democratic institutions.[66]

Carbon sequestration in central Africa is the forest-based environmental service that has received the most international interest. REDD+ (Reducing Emissions from Deforestation and Forest Degradation) is the big item on the agenda. It is a compensation mechanism that has the twofold objective of mitigating climate change by reducing emissions of greenhouse gases and removing greenhouse gases through improved forest management (notably through afforestation and reforestation). Because the DRC has the forest resources the world needs to mitigate global warming, it was the first country in the Congo Basin to benefit from REDD+ financing through the World Bank's Forest Carbon Partnership Facility (FCPF). FCPF has earmarked $60 million in favour of projects – still to be identified – that will achieve the goals set by REDD+. The DRC government, with a helping hand from the United Nations Development Programme, has drafted the conditions under which projects could benefit from such support. Intended areas of implementation are the Kinshasa Basin, the Kisangani Basin and the Mbuji-Mayi/Kananga Basin. The private sector is the preferred sponsor of eligible projects. However, this was just one of many financial commitments. Since 2009, the DRC has also received, from a variety of donors, close to $35 million for REDD-related programmes – to support institutional readiness and capacity-building activities, programme design or project co-funding. In addition, many other programmes or projects funded by the donor community and that cover the farming, forestry or natural resources sectors feature, one way or another, strong REDD or climate change components too.

Pilot projects and studies are being carried out to better understand and act on the drivers of deforestation and forest degradation. A big part of these pilot projects is the design of innovative strategies to compensate people who rely on forests for their livelihoods. Some of the studies defined in Congo's 'REDD readiness plan' focus on improved agricultural strategies, the design and distribution of fuel-efficient cooking stoves, plantation forests and land use planning.[67] This corresponds to Congo's strategy framework that was presented in Doha in 2012 at the International Conference of the Parties on Climate Change. This strategy framework is based on seven themes. Agriculture, energy and forests are the three sector-based themes; governance, demography, land rights and national planning and development are the four transversal ones. From a conceptual perspective, therefore, planners have adopted an integrated approach discourse, but one that seems more perfunctory than pragmatic.

It is still far too early to be able to showcase any REDD+ success stories in Congo. In reality, there is more hype than results, despite the millions of dollars that have been spent – much of which is going to international consultants. REDD+ has little chance of achieving expectations in the Congo and will likely be relegated to the same cemetery where other failed development concepts lie forgotten. Poor governance and weak institutions are the overwhelming prohibiting factors. REDD+ architects have fallen into the trap of adopting a one-size-fits-all template. While REDD+ strategies can work in a country such as Costa Rica, where there are efficient institutions and alternative livelihood options, it cannot work as well in Congo. The land tenure system is not conducive to improving rural populations' farming techniques.[68] Energy needs are not integrated into Congo's REDD+ plans in a realistic way. 'The implementation of REDD+ in DRC will face numerous challenges because of the widespread nature of corruption in the country,' according to some experts.[69] The legal framework needed to make REDD+ work in Congo is inadequate and will require significant legislative reform.[70]

Compensating people to modify their behaviours and change their attitudes also requires a strong bond of trust between government and people in a decentralised and participatory context. Congo lacks these fundamentals. If things are to change, development practitioners struggling to adapt PES to the DRC landscape will have to embed their strategies in the country's political realities and learn from previous attempts at improving forest governance.[71] The current gaps that separate public and private international partners, national authorities and local populations remain wide. If these stakeholders agree on a set of overlapping interests, improved forest governance will still take many years to evolve, and will need continued support from an international community with realistic expectations. It will also require better scientific knowledge and the dynamic involvement of what is today an inefficient civil society.

Most importantly, it will depend of the emergence of far more efficient and transparent state institutions that can convincingly appropriate the need for improved forest governance.

Conclusion: an integrated set of challenges

Congo's forests, full of wealth and mystery, sustain people and contribute to their livelihoods but have hardly enabled them to develop – a major dimension of the environmental paradox. The analysis of the DRC's forest resources highlights inevitable relationships between these resources themselves (such as timber, charcoal, wildlife, carbon and non-timber forest products) and other natural resources, mainly water, minerals and agricultural land. This analysis is based on the argument that forests are inseparable from Congo's broader natural landscape and can best be understood by looking at them in an integrated way.

The examination of forests also sets the tone for the subsequent chapters of this book in terms of the analysis of the political economy of resource use. The strengths – but primarily weaknesses – of the institutional framework, international partnerships, transversal infrastructure priorities, high economic stakes and integration of Congo's forest wealth in the global economy are recurrent themes.

From a conceptual perspective, resolving ambiguous land tenure systems is an institutional challenge, but also a social challenge. Forests are embedded in social contexts that influence how and why people use, depend upon and exploit other resources, such as agricultural land and water. Gender issues and relations between youth and elders are important social matters in forest governance and are factors that influence other resource sectors as well. Traditional authorities play a key (and sometimes controversial) role in governance practices in each of these sectors, and especially in agriculture – the subject of Chapter 3.

Chapter 3

FOOD AND AGRICULTURE

Living off the land

The gap between Congo's potential and development in the agricultural sector is striking. Congo has abundant arable land and an ideal balance of rainfall and sunshine. Its predominantly peasant population has a long tradition of fishing, animal husbandry and the production of diverse cash and subsistence crops. As there is little industry in Congo and few jobs in the formal sectors, two-thirds of the population rely on farming for income and for their daily food. Experts claim that Congo could feed over a billion people – or the equivalent of approximately the entire African continent. Congo has the potential to be the world's seventh most important food producer.[1] These conditions help explain why agriculture has always been the foundation of the Congolese economy. But this foundation is shaky and under pressure from population growth, infrastructure decline, rural migration and ill-adapted legislation. Congo's political system and social context do not appear to be fostering the right kinds of incentives to promote agricultural development in an integrated way. This chapter presents the key factors that need to be considered to conceptually link agriculture with other sectors and with cross-cutting development priorities.

Citing progress in Brazil and China, development economists argue that investment in agriculture is a prerequisite for, first, industrialisation and then overall economic growth. This is a logical pathway for Congo because efficient management of Congo's agricultural resources is not an unrealistic goal. The Belgian Congo could boast a number of real accomplishments in the agricultural sector. These were achieved, however, at a high social cost, ranging from the viciousness of the Leopoldian rubber harvesting phase[2] to the massive expropriation of land[3] and colonial policies forcing peasants to respect agricultural production quotas.[4] Agricultural exports represented 39 per cent of total exports in the late 1950s,[5] but are down to practically zero today. Congo grew more cotton than any other African country and was the world's leading exporter of palm oil following World War II. Unilever, the world's third-largest consumer goods company after Procter & Gamble and Nestlé, owed much of its early success to the Lever Brothers' palm oil concession in Bandundu province. It was established in 1911 to provide the raw material for their soap-making factories in England. The Yangambi agricultural research institute in the heart of the country's tropical rainforest was a world-class centre of excellence in the 1950s. The production of quinine, the only known cure for malaria, is closely associated with the microclimate of the South Kivu highlands.

It will, of course, take many years before this potential can be reached or regained. Once an exporter of food, the DRC now grows too little to meet even the basic nutritional needs of its citizens. Congolese are paradoxically among the hungriest people on earth today. The Economist Intelligence Unit ranks the DRC as the world's most food insecure country, with a score of 107 out of 107 countries surveyed.[6] Congolese children under five years old rank 185 out of 186 in the underweight category.[7] These rankings confirm that food insecurity affects 70 per cent of the population.[8] The average Congolese's dietary energy supply is approximately 1,500 calories per day, far below the 2,500 calories recommended by the Food and Agriculture Organization of the United Nations (FAO). Many mothers cook only one meal per day for their children. Sometimes they have money for food, and sometimes they have money for charcoal, but there are days when they do not have enough for both. Mounds of crops perish in villages, unable to reach markets because of transportation difficulties. Food production increases at a slower annual rate (around 2 per cent) than demographic growth (around 3 per cent), exacerbating hunger prevalence. Salaried work in the agriculture sector, which was common in the colonial period, hardly exists today. Democratisation has the potential to encourage pro-poor agricultural policies in Africa, but this potential has met limited success.[9] The absence of investment in agriculture in Congo may therefore be partially explained by poor results in moving towards the establishment of a real form of democratic governance.

Crops and production

Congo's agricultural potential is underexploited. That gross understatement applies to both subsistence farming and cash crop production. Only 10 per cent of Congo's 800,000 square kilometres of arable land (a surface area larger than France and the United Kingdom combined) is under cultivation. There are, however, considerable regional variations, resulting from access to roads and population density. Favourably diverse climate conditions and types of soil, abundant water and variations in altitude provide a rich agricultural foundation. The county's central basin is suitable for the cultivation of manioc, bananas, rubber, palm oil, coffee and cocoa. The southern savannahs are ideal for growing cereals and beans as well as ranching. They could carry up to 40 million head of cattle, compared with the less than 1 million today.[10] Coffee, tea, quinine, beans, potatoes and cabbage are grown in those mountain regions of eastern Congo so plagued by armed conflict and social trauma. Cheese production has even become a cottage industry in the Goma hinterland since Belgian priests introduced the craft there in the 1970s.

Table 3.1 shows that, cassava – also called manioc – is the most widely consumed food staple in Congo. This could also be considered a paradox because, although cassava is Africa's most common crop (along with maize), it is not indigenous to the continent. It was imported by Portuguese traders from Brazil in the sixteenth century, making it a pioneering globalised commodity. Like an American hamburger or a French Camembert, cassava is very much part of Congo's national identity. The bitter-tasting leaves (which closely resemble cannabis in appearance), prepared with oil, red-hot chilli peppers, onions and sometimes dried or salted fish, are eaten as a vegetable. Each national language has its own term for them: *mpondu* in Lingala, *sombe* in Swahili, *kaleji* in Tshiluba and *sakasaka* in Kikongo. Cassava leaves are highly perishable, however. They do not travel well so they have to be eaten within a few days after being harvested. The ubiquitous cassava root tuber is also a staple food in both rural and urban Congo, prepared primarily as *fufu* and *chikwangue*. The starchy tuber is a good source of carbohydrates but a poor source of protein. It is a filler that helps chase away hunger but without providing much nourishment. Maize flour is sometimes added to cassava flour to make *fufu* depending on availability and cost, and there is an emerging trend to replace cassava *fufu* with imported semolina. While cassava's industrial use has been limited to making laundry starch and animal feed, today international research and investment are exploring its considerable – but controversial – biofuel potential.[11]

Table 3.1 Subsistence agricultural products by province

Province	Cassava	Maize	Rice	Banana	Beans	Groundnuts
Kinshasa	••	••	••	••	••	••
Bandundu	•	•	••	•	••	•
Bas-Congo	•	••	••	•	•	••
Equateur	•	•	•	•	••	•
Kasaï-Occidental	•	•	•	••	•	••
Kasaï-Oriental	•	•	•	••	•	•
Katanga	••	•	••	••	•	•
Maniema	•	•	•	•	••	•
North Kivu	•	•	•	•	•	••
Orientale	•	••	•	•	••	•
South Kivu	•	••	••	•	•	••

* major subsistence production; ** secondary subsistence production.
Sources: Chausse *et al.* (2012); Van Hoof (2011); USAID (2010); Bezy *et al.* (1981).

Table 3.2 Cash crops by province

Province	Palm oil	Rubber	Coffee	Tea	Cotton	Cocoa
Kinshasa	N	N	N	N	N	N
Bandundu	Y	Y	N	N	N	Y
Bas-Congo	Y	Y	Y	N	N	Y
Equateur	Y	Y	Y	N	N	Y
Kasaï-Occidental	Y	A	Y	N	A	N
Kasaï-Oriental	Y	A	N	N	N	N
Katanga	N	N	N	N	A	N
Maniema	Y	N	A	Y	A	N
North Kivu	Y	N	Y	Y	N	N
Orientale	Y	A	Y	N	A	A
South Kivu	Y	N	Y	Y	N	N

Y = yes; N = no; A = production abandoned.
Sources: Chausse *et al.* (2012); Van Hoof (2011); USAID (2010); Bezy *et al.* (1981).

Farming

Slash-and-burn agriculture, also referred to as itinerant, shifting or swidden farming by tropical agronomists, is the principal agrarian system in the dense forests that cover half of Congo's vast territory. In its traditional version, men clear a new field of around 2 or 3 hectares every year with machetes and axes. Gas-powered chainsaws are sometimes available but the use of rudimentary tools prevails. They then set fire to the felled trees and stumps, which produces a thin layer of fertile ash on the topsoil. Women take over in the subsequent time-consuming and back-breaking phases of tilling, planting, weeding, harvesting, carrying, pounding, cooking and selling. A study on farming in South Kivu confirms this gender imbalance: women work 70 per cent more than men.[12]

Traditional local environmental knowledge – sometimes called ethno-ecology – is significant. Peasants combine farming with raising goats, chickens and pigs. The objective of this small-scale animal husbandry is not consumption but the accumulation of bridewealth, ceremonial gifts or 'savings' that can be sold in cases of emergency. It therefore makes a rather insignificant contribution to food security. As rivers and streams are everywhere in the central basin, people fish too. Men also hunt wild animals for food and sale. Bushmeat provides forest dwellers with most of their protein but commercial bushmeat networks organised to supply urban populations with their favourite animals such as duikers, wild boar and monkeys have become unsustainable and a serious threat to biodiversity. Women and children harvest mushrooms, honey, roots and bark for traditional medicines, comestible insects, nuts and berries as well as other non-timber forest products. Agriculture, forests and water resources are accordingly all intertwined.

Although plastic buckets and enamel basins are available in Congo's remote villages, basket weaving is a tradition that is still passed down from mother to daughter – an eco-friendly craft for carrying and storing harvests. Men know which trees are best suited for their mortars and pestles and dugout canoes. Congolese peasants are well versed in rainfall patterns, planting seasons, soil fertility and crop rotation methods. Multiple crops are grown simultaneously to avoid risks from disease and pests. Newly cleared plots are farmed for two or three years. Then, as fertility decreases, they are abandoned to remain fallow for up to ten years before being re-farmed. Yams, taro, maize and groundnuts are the first crops to be planted in new plots because they need more nutrients than the less demanding cassava and bananas that are planted in later cycles.

Slash-and-burn agriculture has been severely criticised in recent years by agronomists and environmentalists who argue that it destroys tropical forests. While this is not entirely false, the criticism needs to be nuanced. Slash-and-burn has been practised for centuries in central Africa, and not only did it not destroy the forests, it contributed to maintaining and enriching their fragile webs of biodiversity. 'Both people and their habitats are part of a single reciprocal system,' according to Jan Vansina, writing in his historical analysis of equatorial Africa.[13] Traditional belief systems confirm this reciprocity. Some communities worship a single spirit for both soil fertility and female fecundity.[14] Others pray to the same deity for animal fertility as well, testifying to their holistic world view.

The problem with slash-and-burn is demographic pressure. While it works well in low population density areas such as Congo's central basin, once the threshold of 20 to 30 people per square kilometre is surpassed, fallow periods become shorter and soil fertility declines. Conflict over land, poaching, illegal small-scale logging and outward migration are the direct consequences. In very high population density areas such as the Kivus or parts of Bas-Congo, slash-and-burn has reached the limits of sustainability.

Food imports

The productivity of food production has declined steadily since the early 1960s. This is the case for subsistence farming but is far more dramatically applicable to cash crops. As Congolese agricultural capacity deteriorated, other countries were revolutionising their food production strategies and boosting productivity rates. It therefore has become cheaper to feed Kinshasa with imported rice (primarily from Thailand, Vietnam and India) than produce it in and transport it from the hinterland. The same can be said for Malaysian cooking oil or American chicken wings. Local production cannot compete with these cheap imports. Congo imports beef from Brazil, South Africa and European Union countries; these imports comprise cuts such as heads, tails and hooves that are undesirable in Europe and the United States – even for pet food. Cost is the overriding factor, but people's tastes and the marketing strategies of multinationals also influence purchasing decisions. Bas-Congo grows, roasts and grinds coffee today. However, in the cities of Boma and Matadi, it is just as easy to find neatly packaged tins of Nescafé in neighbourhood shops as it is to buy local coffee, which is sold in bags made of recycled plastic.

Reliance on imports is a major economic problem but it is an even greater social calamity because no other sector could put as many people to work as food production and processing. Food processing, an important step towards industrialisation, is practically non-existent. The profitable urban fruit juice market benefits South African companies. Congolese women regularly use tomato paste in their cuisine but there is not a single factory in the DRC today that produces it. Until recently it was imported primarily from Italy, but now it increasingly comes from China. The problem concerns not only food processing but consumer products as well. Palm oil harvested in Kivu is hauled to Burundi and Rwanda and returns as soap. Popular brands of soap in Kinshasa have a 'Made in Indonesia' label. Browsing in a Kinshasa supermarket reveals the predominance of imported items. Beer brewing, however, thrives throughout the Congo, proving that industrial-scale production can and does exist – and that it takes money to make money. The business of beer brewing and distribution ranks highly in private sector employment and tax contributions to the Central Bank. Popular brands such as Primus, Mutzig and Turbo King are part of the Dutch Heineken group. Skol, Nkoyi, Castel, Tembo, Simba and Doppel Munich are owned by France's Castel.

Agricultural policies

Economic policies that encouraged capital accumulation through agricultural exploitation were abandoned after independence.[15] They gave way to a lack of vision that continues today. The beginning of the downward spiral came with the broad wave of Mobutu nationalisations in 1973. Zaire's then largest food-producing conglomerate, the Société Générale d'Alimentation, was devastated overnight. Other foreign-owned ranches, fish farms and plantations suffered the same fate.[16] But Mobutu as a food-producing entrepreneur himself did not do badly. In 1977, the Cultures et Élevages du Zaïre conglomerate, which he pieced together from nationalised properties, was Zaire's third-largest employer after the state and the Gécamines mining giant.[17] In the mid-1970s, Mobutu devised a wide range of policies to redress the food security crisis,[18] which he specifically identified as one of Zaire's 'ten plagues', along with social injustice and unemployment.[19] He also set up a number of agencies to promote the production and marketing of commodities such as coffee, cacao, natural rubber and sugar. Some of them still exist today, but more as empty shells than as operational work units. Mobutu opted to invest in mining and prestige infrastructure projects (such as the Inga dam complex and the Inga-Shaba high-tension energy transmission line) to the detriment of agriculture. He did not back up his ambitious agricultural promotion discourse with funding, which accounts for its failure. There were also inconsistencies in his policies: for example, artificially overvaluing the Zaire currency facilitated food imports.

The lootings of the early 1990s and the two wars that shattered lives and the economy from 1996 to 2002 had devastating effects on production and ranching. President Laurent-Désiré Kabila never really had the opportunity to promote agriculture because much of his time at the helm of the nation was devoted to the war effort – and to making shady deals in the mining sector to pay for it. President Joseph Kabila has also focused on mining without encouraging the government or investors to give adequate attention to food production. There has also been insufficient investment in agricultural research and training.[20] The misguided tax system privileges imports instead of local production. The inexorable disintegration of transport infrastructure and poor distribution networks exacerbate these problems.[21]

As the country emerged from war, Congo's international partners designed and funded all kinds of state-building initiatives but they too neglected agriculture. With so many other urgent needs to address, their focus was on reform of the security sector, economy and public finance, improved governance and rule of law, and the physical rehabilitation of infrastructure. However, some important donors, such as the United States Agency for International Development (USAID) and the European Commission, have specific projects targeting improved food security. Others, such as Belgian Technical Cooperation, fund initiatives that benefit farmers; these include work on rehabilitating rural feeder roads. In the past decade, international partners have spent between $100 million and $150 million per year on agriculture.[22] For comparison, the United Nations peacekeeping and stabilisation operation in Congo (MONUSCO) costs $1.5 billion per year.

A host of policy papers, strategic documents and laws devoted to agriculture have been drawn up in post-conflict Congo by the government and international partners. In 2006, the government prepared a strategic document that identified agricultural development as a priority to contribute to poverty reduction (*Document de stratégie pour la réduction de la pauvreté*). In 2010, the government adopted an official strategic plan for agriculture and rural development (*Stratégie sectorielle de l'agriculture et du développement rural*). An agricultural finance and investment programme was launched at the end of 2013 to modernise agriculture, coordinate funding and plan for costs up until 2020 (*Programme national d'investissement agricole*). The government also established the Société de Parcs Agro-industriels, a public–private partnership managed by the South African company Mozfood & Energy, whose objective is to promote private sector investment.[23] It is too early to evaluate these initiatives because they are recent creations, but on the level of discourse, they reveal an acceptance of an integrated approach.

President Kabila signed into law a new Agricultural Code in December 2011 (*Loi portant principes fondamentaux relatifs à l'agriculture*), which responded to a serious policy gap. Congo had lacked a comprehensive agricultural policy framework for several decades, just as it did in other sectors such as mining and forestry. In an attempt to address this policy vacuum, the Code sets outs general guidelines. Its stated purpose is to promote and increase agricultural production to ensure food security and rural development. Provisions apply to food production, training and research, taxation and customs, financing, marketing and environmental protection. It does not apply to livestock, fisheries and aquaculture, however, which undermines its capacity to deal sufficiently with food security issues.

Application of the law is contingent upon two unavoidable prerequisites. One is respect for the decentralisation process outlined in the Constitution. Agricultural policy, according to the law, must be implemented at the national, provincial and local levels, involving stakeholders from the government, civil society and the private sector. But decentralisation has not been given adequate political attention and is on hold, a situation that has direct negative consequences for the implementation of the agriculture law. The second problem pertains to the slow progress made in elaborating the law's operational by-laws. These are needed to stipulate funding and taxation issues and the rights and responsibilities of the different stakeholders. A general framework will not be enough to meet targets without these by-laws.

Although President Kabila signed the law on 24 December, it was not a Christmas present for foreign investors. Article 16 explicitly restricts foreigners' access to farmlands. Reminiscent of the Mobutu nationalisations, it requires majority ownership by Congolese nationals. Foreign investors and the Congolese Federation of Enterprises are advocating for amendments to Article 16 because it is a real disincentive and vitiates other government policies aimed at encouraging foreign private investment. The controversial ownership article was included because of concerns about land grabbing. In a context of weak sovereign control over resources and territory, it is not illogical to try to foresee and circumscribe threats to land use and ownership.

Although the government signed the Maputo Declaration[24] in 2003, it has devoted only between 1 and 2 per cent of the national budget to the sector in recent years. The little money that is available in this envelope is largely spent on salaries in Kinshasa with minimal trickle-down into the field. More than 95 per cent of state-employed agronomists and veterinarians work in Kinshasa or in the provincial capitals.[25] Like the forest and water sectors, agriculture is far from being a real priority for key decision makers in Congo today. The absence of government funding is one indicator of this. The fact that parliament does not have a permanent agricultural commission is another.

On the institutional landscape, there is an overall lack of professionalism and capacity in terms of human resources and material. Government offices responsible for agricultural priorities are underfunded, understaffed and in need of competent experts with up-to-date professional skills and vision. They also lack data management systems and basic equipment such as filing cabinets, copiers and computers, let alone internet access. An additional hurdle is the number of ministries involved in managing the sector. The Ministry of Agriculture, the Ministry of Rural Development, the Ministry of Environment Conservation, Water and Forests, the Ministry of Scientific and Technological Research and the Ministry of Women and the Family all share rural development and agricultural responsibilities. In theory, the Ministry of Planning coordinates the financing of these five ministries but, in reality, it is overwhelmed with other urgent issues. The problem here is that when priorities are supposed to be dealt with by multiple partners, responsibility essentially lies with none of them – so no one really does anything. There is an absence of coordination, tasks get passed on to someone else, disagreements arise over costs, and there tends to be a generalised absence of accountability and ownership.

Urbanisation and food

Urbanisation in Congo, as in most other African countries, has been a postcolonial process. Population movement under Belgian rule was strictly controlled. The indigenous labour force was organised to produce food and export crops, dig in the mines or toil at public works infrastructure development. The establishment of the head tax in the 1920s – and harsh punishment for not paying it – kept people working. Until independence, the vast majority of Congolese lived and worked in rural areas. Access to the city was reserved to a select few who found jobs as house servants, shop assistants or clerks.

This has changed dramatically: people do whatever they can to leave their villages or arrange for their children to do so. Despite the difficulties in finding work, food and housing in the big cities, people see them as offering more hope for the future than their villages, where access to health clinics and schools, water and electricity, cold beer, entertainment and elegant dress is still a very long way off. Young men and women prefer the relative anonymity of even the urban slum compared with the strict kinship codes that govern village life. The fear of witchcraft sanctions is yet another motivation to escape what is perceived as being a place with no future. The city is also seen as a stepping stone to Europe or America. As a consequence, there has been steady outward rural migration since independence, resulting in an urban–rural ratio of approximately 35–65 today. Kinshasa alone has a population of 10 million, meaning that about one Congolese in seven lives there. The overcrowded melting pots of Lubumbashi, Matadi, Mbuji-Mayi, Kananga, Kisangani, Kolwezi, Goma and Bukavu need to be fed but production and supply lag behind demand.

Urbanisation has direct impacts on agriculture and food supply networks. Rural outward migration results in a process that has been described as 'de-agrarianisation', which in simple terms means that people are abandoning their fields.[26] Demographic shifts can disrupt food production, but do not necessarily do so. Although only 2 per cent of the American population work in agriculture, they are able to produce abundant surpluses; conversely, the declining agricultural workforce in Congo means that there is less food. Fewer people farm for an ever growing population in a non-industrialised, under-mechanised and hostile economic environment with deplorably inadequate transportation and storage infrastructure. Arbitrary taxation and harassment by greedy officials and men with guns are further disincentives for peasants to grow surplus crops for sale.[27]

Urban and peri-urban food production is a major trend that has accompanied the urbanisation process. The urban poor produce food in and around all of Congo's cities, with Kinshasa taking the lead. Underpaid civil servants and/or their wives form a large corps of peri-urban farmers. It is not uncommon to see them shuttling between town and field with a mobile phone in one hand and a machete or hoe in the other. Cassava and maize are the main crops in these areas too. The ways in which crops are produced differentiate rural techniques from those developed in peri-urban areas. Some examples include the size of the plot, organic composting, the use of improved seeds, insecticides and chemical fertilisers that are acquired in town, and the short duration of fallow periods.

Peri-urban agriculture takes place in three main types of space: 1) farming within the house lot (*parcelle*), also known as kitchen gardening; 2) just beyond the village limits; and 3) increasingly, as a consequence of soil fatigue, further and further into the village outskirts referred to as *nzamba* (forest). The types of crops grown and their ultimate use (sale or family consumption) determine where they will be grown. Vegetables for household consumption are grown on the *parcelle* and are supplemented by staples grown beyond the village limits. Market gardening (*maraîchage*) takes place on permanent plots close to the village to grow tomatoes, leeks, celery, cabbage, carrots and spring onions for sale in Kinshasa. Farming in the *nzamba* is also largely destined for commercial purposes and takes place on large plots of up to approximately 1 hectare. In all of these cases, work is labour intensive and is carried out with rudimentary tools. A fourth category of peri-urban agricultural space is the 'plantation'. Urban elites who appropriate large concessions for themselves through political manoeuvring own these considerably larger plots and exploit them exclusively for commercial purposes.

Animal husbandry is also part of the peri-urban food supply strategy. Pigs and chickens primarily, but also ducks, are raised in conditions that range from village-like practices where animals roam around freely and feed themselves to semi-industrialised systems where they are bred in pens or cages and nourished with commercially purchased feed and treated with industrial veterinary products. As semi-industrialised farms are relatively expensive to acquire, protect and maintain, they tend to be the initiatives of politically well-connected urban elites. Fish farming (mainly of tilapia and catfish) and increasing examples of the small-scale breeding of cane rats and guinea pigs can also be observed. Theft is a serious problem and undermines these initiatives. It ranges from a worker pilfering a few fish or a small quantity of manioc leaves to looting by hungry soldiers with guns. Both examples are significant disincentives to invest in peri-urban areas.

It is difficult to say exactly where the city ends and where the peri-urban space begins.[28] There is also, according to Bryceson, a lot of 'fussiness' in delineating administrative and operational boundaries.[29] Nevertheless, it is certain that feeding Kinshasa has social, economic and environmental impacts that start at the immediate outskirts of the city and extend up to 500 kilometres into Bas-Congo and Bandundu. The large number of overloaded lorries, pick-ups and cars along the main supply roads that link Boma–Matadi–Kinshasa and Kikwit–Kinshasa is an obvious indicator. Sacks of food and loose stalks of plantain bananas are deposited at Kinshasa's main markets[30] but sometimes at 'phantom' markets or gathering areas where buyers and sellers meet surreptitiously to avoid tax officials. A polygamist entrepreneur revealed an innovative form of food production and sale to me: he has one wife in the hinterland who grows food for him and another wife in town who sells it.

Mining and agriculture

Urbanisation is the primary reason why farmers leave their land, but it is not the only one. Small-scale artisanal mining is also a major incentive for young men to lay down their machetes and axes and pick up shovels and sieves. The phenomenon is widespread in many mineral-rich countries and involves millions of rural people.[31] Access to mineral deposits close to the surface and the activity's low entry costs make for a tempting alternative to farming. Repercussions on food production are automatic. Bezy *et al.* were among the first to record this problem in Kasaï-Oriental resulting from diamond mining.[32] Stephen Jackson makes a similar connection: 'At the height of coltan fever, a sharp decline in food security in the Masisi was felt as young men quit agricultural production to chase dollars.'[33] He also draws attention to a classic Dutch disease syndrome: as coltan prices soared, so did the price of manioc because it was imported instead of being produced locally.[34]

From a gender perspective, it is not easy to account for the relationship between artisanal mining and the decline in food production. Although it is generally believed that women do most of the farming work and men provide most of the artisanal mining labour, in reality women also lay down their farming tools to work in and around the mines – and not only as prostitutes, which is an inappropriate stereotype. Just as gender roles are clearly defined in farming, they are too in artisanal mining. Women carry out the crucial steps of cleaning and washing the sludge dug by men and then bagging and transporting the ore.

While some people leave their villages and plots by choice, others are constrained to do so. Armed conflict has displaced millions of people, particularly in North and South Kivu but also in the provinces of Orientale, Equateur and Katanga. There were an estimated 2.6 million internally displaced Congolese in mid-2013[35] – down from a peak of 3.5 million at the end of the war in late 2002. These cases of forced displacement have severe negative effects on food security.

Land grabbing

Land grabbing is not new to Africa or to the Congo – only the term itself is. King Leopold's concession policies in the Congo Free State were an early example of this form of predation. The vacant land legislation (*terres vacantes et sans maître*) effectively dispossessed people of their ancestral lands.[36] Leopold's agents decided that if land was not being used, it could be appropriated for reasons of the 'civilising mission'. Large-scale land concessions were consolidated by colonial development policies, a situation that lingered on until Mobutu implemented the Bakajika law in 1973, a law that sought to regain state sovereignty over land. A rather bizarre postcolonial concession was negotiated in 1976. Mobutu leased 98,000 square kilometres of Katanga province (around the size of the American state of Vermont) to West Germany's Orbital Transport and Rocket Corporation as a rocket-launching site and test range.[37] OTRAG was to enjoy full sovereignty over the land and 'could call upon the Zairian government to evacuate all persons ... from the area'.[38] This was a foreboding of the land-grabbing schemes that would subsequently befall Africa. These patterns of dispossession, domination and repression confirm the point of view that the politics of land acquisition take place in 'arenas of confrontation and negotiation'.[39]

Large-scale land acquisition is indeed a phenomenon that has been taking place in much of Africa over the past decade as capital-poor countries seek to attract foreign capital: 'agricultural development centred on large-scale land investments has become the reigning paradigm'.[40] Nonetheless, the land-grabbing deals that many civil society activists feared do not appear to have occurred in the DRC – at least not yet. Acquirers target lands that are well irrigated and fertile (which Congo has) and lands in areas that have transportation infrastructures and electricity (which Congo does not have). There is relatively little interest in large-scale ranching in Congo, in part because diseases such as trypanosomiasis, which is transmitted by tsetse flies, are constraints. However, some deals with big multinationals have been secured. Feronia of Canada (controlled by Indian multi-billionaire C. Sivasankaran) acquired 100,000 hectares of oil palm concessions from Unilever in 2009. The three concessions – Yaligimba and Boteka in Equateur province and Lokutu in Orientale – are near the Congo River upon which barges transport palm nuts to Kinshasa to be refined. Feronia also has a 10,000-hectare concession in Bas-Congo where it grows rice. His Excellency Kikaya-Bin-Karubi, the DRC's ambassador to the United Kingdom, sat on Feronia's board of directors.[41] There was considerable speculation about a huge land acquisition by China's telecommunications giant ZTE (the world's fourth-largest manufacturer of mobile phones). The company was granted a 100,000-hectare concession for palm oil production but has not moved ahead with the project. The scheme remained 'moribund' because Chinese officials 'believed the transport costs would be too high in the DRC to make the project profitable'.[42] ZTE's activities are limited to two relatively small experimental farming concessions in the Kinshasa hinterland. A German private equity fund, DWS Global Agricultural Land and Opportunities Fund, has a 25,000-hectare farming concession.

At this stage, a greater land-grabbing threat comes from within than from abroad. Powerful Congolese and expatriates have been actively appropriating concessions for themselves, most often in peri-urban areas. The politically well-connected have the administrative savvy and financial means necessary to gain written title to land, often to the detriment of local communities who rely on oral arrangements with traditional chiefs to access land. President Kabila has a number of farms: the 300-hectare Ferme de l'Espoir near Lubumbashi, his farm at Kingakati near Kinshasa, and a concession north of Bukavu. Moïse Katumbi, a former Katanga governor and successful businessman, has his multiple-use Futuka farm 70 kilometres from Lubumbashi where he carries out food production (crops, livestock and fish farming), agricultural training

and eco-tourism. Former Security and Justice Minister Jeannot
Mwenze Kongolo and the disgraced former Chief of the National
Police Force John Numbi also have large swathes of land outside
Lubumbashi. The man who sat next to President Kabila at Augustin
Katumba Mwanke's funeral, Israeli businessman Dan Gertler, set
up the Gertler Family Foundation which runs the Kitoko Food
Farm at N'sele. While the stated objective of the Kitoko farm is the
sustainable development of commercial farming, it would be naïve
not to see the venture as a means of securing access to land that
is steadily increasing in value due to its proximity to sub-Saharan
Africa's second-largest city. Gertler has already invested heavily in
mining and oil in the DRC and is alleged to have been involved in
some rather shady investment deals.[43] While the Canadian, Chinese
and German deals mentioned above lend support to Saskia Sassen's
argument that 'land ... has become one of the major new needs of
advanced capitalism',[44] land acquisition by the politically powerful
Congolese and their cronies appears to be more of an ongoing
manifestation of patrimonial politics.

Palm oil is one of Congo's agricultural commodities that
deserves particular attention because of its potential to interest
multinational land grabbers. Versatile and comparatively cheap, it
is an ingredient in numerous food and non-food items sold in an
average supermarket. Margarine, cereals, crisps, sweets and baked
goods are a few examples; soaps, washing detergents, body creams
and cosmetics are others. Nutella and Kellogg's Frosted Flakes would
not taste the same without it. Palm oil is also used in animal feed and
as a biofuel, which also explains its increasing international demand.
It has become the world's cheapest and most widely consumed
vegetable fat. But oil palms grow only in tropical environments
close to the equator, making Congo a prime candidate for new (and
rehabilitated) plantations. Malaysia and Indonesia are the main
producers: oil palm production is a main driver of deforestation
in both of these countries. The world's largest palm oil producer,
Sime Darby of Malaysia, has set its sights on Africa and has already

acquired a large concession in Liberia, where thousands of people are being displaced.[45] Another giant, Singapore-based Olam, has a huge 300,000-kilometre concession in Gabon.[46] There is consequently a strong likelihood that industrial oil palm production will expand towards the Congo in the coming years. Congo's poor governance record and complicated land tenure system, combined with the overall non-transparent nature of land acquisition deals throughout Africa, highlight the need for scepticism about farmers' rights, given the commercial value of palm oil.[47]

The land-grabbing debate is somewhat similar to the one going on about the advantages and disadvantages of biofuels. For proponents, biofuels are a sustainable, green and reliable energy alternative. With more research and technology, it could be possible to overcome social and environmental disadvantages and make them suitable for widespread consumer use. One of the main arguments advanced by detractors, however, is that using land for biofuel crops means less land for growing food. They further contend that it is unethical to use land for biofuel when hunger is a worldwide problem. This could even be considered a violation of basic human rights. In some instances, the marketplace appears to be in favour of biofuels. 'The combination of higher and more volatile commodity and oil prices, population growth and urbanization, globalization and climate change is likely to imply that biofuel demand and investments will be of even greater importance in the future,' according to Matondi et al.[48] Demand is on the rise in the United States, Brazil and some countries of the European Union – the three big biofuel markets. For the United States, biofuels derived from the maize fields of the American Midwest diminish the country's dependency on foreign oil. Brazil uses sugar cane-based fuels as a cost-effective means of driving its economic growth: they cover approximately a quarter of its road transport fuel, for example.[49] The European Commission sees biofuels as being politically correct, defending the view that they are a sustainable low-carbon source of energy that will help meet European commitments to fight against global climate change. As a result, Europe requires a certain amount of energy to come from renewable sources such as biofuels.[50]

Congo has the land and climate to grow massive quantities of maize, sugar cane, soya beans, cassava and other crops with biofuel potential. As it has large tracts of land that lie outside its rainforests, the problems of deforestation experienced in other countries could be avoided. Biofuels could also help solve some of Congo's energy needs, especially in remote rural areas where there is neither electricity nor readily available petrol. The technology needed to convert agricultural feedstock into biofuel is not very sophisticated and could be made available. The main challenge here is the absence of relevant policies, funding, regulatory frameworks and administrative capacity. The land-for-biofuel issue also highlights the fact that important political economy priorities are decided upon not by the Congolese themselves but by foreign actors and global dynamics.

Marketing and innovations

Mobile phone use took off in Congo in the late 1990s. It transformed society in general while also providing a much-needed boost to food production and marketing. It helped communities organise collective transportation, which reduced costs and increased security. Farmers became better informed of price fluctuations and market opportunities so were less likely to be taken advantage of by unscrupulous traders and intermediaries. The mobile continues to revolutionise access to banking services such as credit and payments, which still constitute bottlenecks in commodity chains. Today, the relatively inexpensive motorcycle made in India or China is the social innovation that is contributing to change in the lives of rural farmers, especially those who live in isolated communities far from feeder roads.

The eastern Congolese cities of Butembo, Bunia, Goma and Bukavu first introduced motorcycles for private transport in the 1990s and then as taxis in 2002. Usage has spread rapidly throughout the country. One student from Kisangani used his motorcycle to take cigarettes and used clothing into mining zones and traded them for gold. These profitable operations allowed him to acquire the money he needed to finish his university studies but he was fearful of his security so abandoned the trade, claiming that: 'The money wasn't worth risking my life.'[51] His friends traded salt and sugar for smoked fish in the Kisangani hinterland thanks to their motorcycles. Reluctant at first, Kinshasa's population has now embraced the taxi motorcycle for its efficiency in navigating the capital's increasingly congested streets. Its advantages seem to outweigh the inconvenience of dust, bad weather and the risk of accident.

These easily maintained motorcycles are cost effective and well adapted to the laterite tracks that crisscross Congo's rural landscape, even during the rainy season. As poor road infrastructure is one of the major handicaps for getting crops to market, the motorcycle is a welcome novelty. The heavily laden bicycle is still a familiar means of carrying produce, although a slow and exhausting form of labour. It is increasingly common, nonetheless, to see a young man on a motorcycle with a bag of cassava, a plastic jug of palm oil or even a pig or a goat en route to an intermediary market accessible to pick-up trucks or large lorries.

As the purchasing power of the young villager is weak, coming up with the approximately $1,200 to buy a 125cc motorcycle is beyond the reach of most. But young men hanker after them, seeing them as an undeniable symbol of modernity, prestige and liberty. Some Congolese believe that the sudden appearance of motorcycles is a witchcraft phenomenon – people enter into pacts with sorcerers to acquire the coveted two-wheelers by sacrificing family members.

Many of the motorcycles plying Congo's rural tracks are purchased by traders who advance payment for them in exchange for promises of agricultural goods. Young men thus enter into a kind of indentured servitude to pay off their debts. Although the motorcycle's impact is slight in terms of agricultural marketing, this is an emerging positive trend whose ramifications are difficult to predict. Most development planners in the late 1980s dismissed projects to supply food to Kinshasa by river, focusing on the more fashionable road transport. Thanks to wooden boats built in Bandundu, however, these *balenières* now carry a significant share of the food consumed in the capital.[52] This point serves to reinforce how difficult it is to predict trends in socially volatile environments. While the motorcycle is unlikely to contribute significantly to feeding Congo's towns and cities, it is nevertheless already augmenting rural revenues.

Other agrarian innovations are also emerging in the DRC that offset – however slightly for the moment – the negative impacts of productivity decline and de-agrarianisation. One is agroforestry, which is a multipurpose practice endorsed by conservation non-governmental organisations (NGOs) and food security programmes. Promoted as 'climate-smart agriculture', agroforestry is considered a sustainable alternative to slash-and-burn, especially in high population density areas. It increases food and fuelwood production while reducing pressure on remaining forest areas and it can be successful in regenerating degraded savannah lands. It helps maintain or enhance soil fertility and combats soil erosion. The logic is relatively simple: farmers are encouraged to plant food crops in association with fast-growing tree species – acacia in most cases. Tree leaves (used as compost) and roots enrich the soil, which increases crop yields. Associating pig, goat and cattle breeding provides an added advantage because the brush that grows under the trees can be used as fodder. Manure, in turn, is used as a crop fertiliser. Once the trees attain a certain height and width (after around eight years), they are cut down to produce cooking charcoal. With the sale of the charcoal, farmers can purchase improved seeds, pesticides and fertilisers, again improving their yields. Beekeeping in acacia forests is another added advantage because it produces a nicely scented honey whose sale supplements incomes.

Variations of this ostensibly attractive system are carried out in many African countries. In the DRC, they are practised in the provinces of Bandundu and Bas-Congo, which supply Kinshasa with cassava, corn and bananas, as well as cooking charcoal. A large project funded by the European Commission in Mampu, 150 kilometres outside Kinshasa on the sandy soils of the Batéké Plateau, is a good illustration of the advantages of agroforestry. Not only does it provide stable employment to farmers but it has also regenerated plant and animal biodiversity. Most importantly, it helps Kinshasa with its inexorable charcoal dependency. At one point, the Mampu project contributed between 5 and 10 per cent of Kinshasa's charcoal needs,[53] but this percentage has decreased because production remains stable while the city's population is increasing. It is nonetheless a significant contribution that helps both people and the environment. The success of Mampu results from its proximity to a main road. Similar projects are planned for Lubumbashi, the Virungas, Kisangani, Kananga and Mbuji-Mayi.

Agroforestry does, of course, have political and cultural drawbacks. Rural populations have to be convinced of its merits before changing their traditional farming techniques and are reluctant to 'invest in agroforestry unless there are adequate incentives'.[54] Timing is an obstacle because it takes two to three years before any tangible results are achieved and it can take many years for the messages of awareness campaigns to be appropriated. Land rights have to be secured too, which is an ongoing battle. Alain Karsenty, a leading expert on African land tenure challenges, has concisely summarised this complex problem: 'In DRC, the forest land tenure system is characterized by a compromise between the 1973 land tenure law (Bakajika law) under Mobutu's rule, which nationalized all land in the former Zaire, and the pragmatism of lawmakers who are well aware of the prevalence of customary rights and the power of traditional chiefs throughout the territory.'[55]

The system also requires technical assistance from qualified experts to teach farmers how to take full advantage of agroforestry opportunities. NGO and internationally funded project staff provide this expertise because it is a priority for them, and because

the Congolese government does not have the capacity or willingness to do so.

Agricultural empowerment

The kind of large-scale land acquisitions taking place elsewhere in
Africa will likely increase smallholder vulnerability in rural and peri-
urban Congo. This disenfranchisement, combined with negative
perceptions of rural life, motivates the inexorable movement of
young fortune seekers towards the city. De-agrarianisation, in
turn, translates into more food imports. As population density
increases, traditional farming practices contribute to deforestation,
biodiversity loss and other forms of environmental stress such as
soil depletion and fuelwood scarcity. National agricultural policies,
so far, have proven unable to accommodate the expectations of
rural communities and the dynamics of globalisation. Researchers
and NGOs have contributed significantly to understanding how
agriculture contributes to deforestation, but, again, the government
has not been able to capitalise on this new understanding to move
ahead with specific policy recommendations related to carbon
trading or REDD+ (Reducing Emissions from Deforestation and
Forest Degradation), for example.

There is strong evidence that Congo's rural populations are
caught in a poverty trap. Traditional agricultural practices allow
most rural populations to feed themselves, but not to develop.
Without a major overhaul of transport infrastructure, they will not
be able to get their crops to market. Lacking access to credit, they
will not be able to invest in seeds, pesticides or fertilisers. Deprived
of secure title to land, they will continue to suffer from uncertainty,
vulnerability and, in extreme cases, forceful exclusion from their
ancestral lands. People may have land but little more – and their
claims to it are under threat. Nonetheless, insufficient investment in
rural development by the Congolese government and international
partners is not necessarily an irreversible pattern. There are some

positive trends emerging from the rural world, where civil society associations are increasingly well organised and working towards a shared vision for rural empowerment. A long history of vulnerability has taught people to be resilient and creative in a spirit of pragmatic solidarity. Most innovation in African agriculture takes place in areas that have high population density or that have experienced severe environmental stress. It is not surprising, therefore, that the Congolese civil society most active in agricultural empowerment is to be found in the Kivus.

Congolese civil society played a positive role in the drafting of the 2011 agriculture law (a long process of negotiation with significant support from international NGOs) and is active in the National Commission for Land Reform (Commission Nationale de la Réforme Foncière). There is institutional progress too. Village-level farmers' organisations are developing synergies with local development and conservation committees and interact with the Confederation of Congolese Peasant Organisations (CONAPAC). Agricultural management counsels (*conseils agricoles de gestion*) have also been set up. Provincial platforms and federations facilitate cooperative initiatives, access to micro-credit, basic legal advice, transportation and advocacy for education and training that is relevant to rural communities. These initiatives are largely people-based with the support of sympathetic international NGOs. People are aware that the government will not do much to help them. But at least the government is not hostile to these developments – probably because they are essentially apolitical. The Congolese state brutally crushes political civil society movements but appears indifferent to the strategies and actions implemented by rural populations to take better charge of their own destinies.

Agriculture: a total social fact

Agriculture is intimately connected to forest degradation in Congo, but, as this chapter has indicated, it also has obvious links with other fundamental development priorities. These include transportation, institutional and policy frameworks, artisanal mining regulation, access to credit and measures to protect people's rights in the global scramble for African land. Agriculture is therefore at the crux of the debate on stakeholder rights and responsibilities – mainly those of the state, farmers, traditional authorities and international companies. Despite the rapidly changing global context of food and agriculture and increased pressure on Congo's arable land, this debate is still largely unresolved. As in other environmental sectors, there is a lack of political vision with respect to agriculture. The result is that rural populations are left to fend for themselves and city dwellers go hungry.

These problems highlight the relevancy of an integrated approach to agricultural development within the broader goals of macroeconomic strategies. Given the new dynamics in Congolese and African agriculture, the sector or 'silo' approach will prove to be increasingly obsolete.[56] Indeed, more and more experts have come to advocate for 'integrated strategies for sustainable agricultural development that consider food needs as encompassing more than nutrition and food security but also drawing from culture, community practices and local knowledge'.[57] Russell *et al.* make a strong case for the need to integrate agriculture and forestry policies for improved conservation and protected area management efforts throughout the Congo Basin.[58] Congolese agriculture – and land use practices in general – can therefore be considered a 'total social fact' à la Marcel Mauss, which refers to activities that have far-reaching implications throughout society, extending to the economic, legal, political and religious domains. This focus on interconnectivities and interdependencies is perfectly relevant to the social, political and economic needs of the DRC and its people – but probably unrealistic in the current phase of stabilisation and state building.

Chapter 4

WATER: AN UNCERTAIN EBB AND FLOW

Africa's richest watershed

Water is another great resource paradox in the Congo. While the country has more than half of all of Africa's lakes, rivers, streams and wetlands, only a small percentage of Congolese have access to clean drinking water. This giant of a country has the hydroelectric potential to light up the entire continent but less than 9 per cent of the Congolese population is connected to the national power grid. The right to water is granted by the Constitution – and was a Millennium Development Goal – but it is also an intolerable gender problem. A young girl with a yellow plastic water jug on her head is a haunting sight throughout the country's cities and villages. Her water chores often have priority over school attendance. Despite favourable conditions for catching and producing fish, and strong cultural preferences for eating it, fishing and fish farming have not helped improve the country's poor food security situation. 'Water is life' – the slogan of the national water board – but it also brings death. Water-borne intestinal diseases are a major cause of infant mortality. Torrential rains regularly kill people, washing out roads and destroying homes through flooding, landslides and gully erosion. The mythical Mamy Wata water spirit epitomises the Congo River: mysterious, unfathomable, seductive, full of life … but deadly.

This chapter presents the astonishing wealth and diversity of Congo's water resources, including its hydroelectric potential and transportation value. Drinking water and sanitation challenges, the vulnerability of natural fish stocks and the decline of fish farming are also discussed. While water is the main theme, the focus here is on the specific subsectors that have varying degrees of interconnectivity among themselves and links with the resources presented in other chapters. The concluding section on governance discusses a set of recurring problems. Water could be a driver of economic and social development and could also play a role in maintaining the natural environment, but the macroeconomic context and ill-defined institutional frameworks are not favourable at the present time. Like forests and agriculture, water helps sustain people but does not contribute to their development.

The Congo Basin is by far the largest in Africa: it is much bigger than the Nile and Lake Chad basins. In addition to the DRC, it extends across eight other countries: most of the Republic of Congo, the Central African Republic, eastern Zambia, northern Angola, Rwanda, Burundi and parts of Cameroon and Tanzania. The Congo Basin, 62 per cent of which lies in the DRC, has 23 per cent of Africa's irrigation potential – so vital for agriculture.[1] There is a symbiotic relationship between the Basin's vast wetlands and the DRC's abundant rainfall. Average annual rainfall in the DRC is 1,646 millimetres,[2] compared with 1,466 in Brazil.[3] There is, in turn, a direct association between these amazing water resources and Congo's biodiversity-rich tropical forests. Each one contributes to the fragile maintenance of the other. This relationship supports the appeal for an integrated management vision.

The Basin's river network, the densest in the world, is an integral part of what makes life work in the Congo. The country is dominated by the emblematic Congo River, referred to as 'the river that swallows all rivers' by the peoples of Bas-Congo; it is the world's second most important river by volume of flow and one of the longest and deepest. Rising in the highlands of the East African Rift in the vicinity of lakes Tanganyika and Mweru, it flows 4,700 kilometres to the Atlantic coast. At Stanley Pool, located slightly upstream from

Kinshasa, it has an average flow of 38,000 cubic metres a second.[4] Its flow is quite stable for two main ecological reasons. First, there is always at least one part of the river experiencing a rainy season because its drainage basin straddles the equator on the north and south sides. Second, the sandy formations of the large Bandundu Plateau contain an important underground water table that drains into the Kasaï River (a tributary of the Congo River) even in the dry season. Figure 4.1 shows Congo's more than 30 main tributaries with their 20,000 kilometres of riverbanks[5] – astonishingly, this is equivalent to the distance between the North and South poles. Some of this fresh water comes from springs, most of it from rain.

Figure 4.1 Drainage map of the DRC

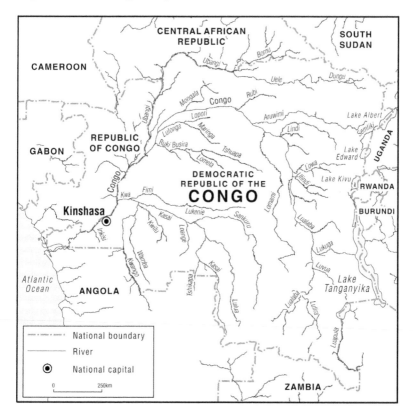

The country derives its name from that of the river, highlighting its importance as an identity-defining resource. The river had major importance in the Mobutu *authenticité* doctrine. The post-colony he imagined was free and strong thanks to the three Zs: Zaire the country, Zaire the river and Zaire the currency. Joseph Conrad saw the river as a 'giant snake' leading into darkness. Thierry Michel suggests, conversely, that the river can lead the country out of darkness and stagnation – which is overly optimistic in the current context.[6] Robert Harms captured its contradictory nature by describing it as both a 'river of wealth' and a 'river of sorrow'.[7]

Globalisation started in central Africa in the sixteenth century, facilitated by the Congo River. Slaves for the New World, and then ivory and rubber, were traded in a downstream direction in exchange for European goods penetrating into the upstream hinterland. The Portuguese, who discovered the Congo Estuary in 1482, had a strong claim to it at the time of the Berlin Conference in 1885. Portugal was indeed granted territories on both the right and left banks: Angola as a colony and Cabinda as a protectorate. Leopold's clever diplomacy of promising access to all countries for trade throughout the Congo Free State was replicated specifically for unrestricted access to the Congo River and its tributaries. This was established by the Navigation Act, which was elaborated in the broader context of the colonial partition of Africa.[8]

Congo's abundant waters are a blessing in many respects, but they are also the source of latent diplomatic nightmares. As access to water increasingly becomes one of humanity's fundamental preoccupations, water diplomacy could be a new challenge to Congo's relations with its neighbours. 'Water is one of the 21st century's most sought-after assets and is shaping and fuelling some of Africa's current (and probably future) conflicts on an alarming scale,' according to Nir Kalron.[9] His warning helps put Table 4.1 into perspective, with its far-reaching geopolitical implications.

Table 4.1 Congo's cross-border waters and concerns

Body of water	Shared with	Concerns
Congo River Estuary	Angola	Oil***, disputed border***
Congo River	Republic of Congo	Water transfer+
Ubangi River	Central African Republic	Water transfer+, hydropower+
Kwango River	Angola	Diamond fields**
Kasaï River	Angola	Diamond fields*
Ruzizi River	Burundi and Rwanda	Hydropower**, oil+, disputed border+
Lake Tanganyika	Burundi, Tanzania and Zambia	Water management**, conservation**, fishing practices*, oil+, pollution+, disputed border (*with Zambia, + with Burundi)
Lake Mweru	Zambia	Fishing practices**
Lake Kivu	Rwanda	Methane gas**, disputed border***
Lake Edward	Uganda	Oil***, disputed border***, fishing practices**, pollution+
Lake Albert	Uganda	Oil***, disputed border***, fishing practices**, pollution+

*** significant; ** secondary; * minor; + potential.
Source: Research synthesis.

The Interbasin Water Transfer project reveals how Congo's water has aroused keen international attention – but not necessarily in the best interests of the Congo and the Congolese. It is a good example of an infrastructure development fantasy with potentially high environmental costs. Lake Chad has shrunk over the past decades because of changing rainfall patterns, drought and human-induced deforestation. Its size is only one-tenth of what it was in the 1960s.[10] This has had dramatic social, economic and environmental consequences. Trying to restore the lake is therefore of paramount importance to the entire Chad Basin region. The Interbasin Water Transfer project is an idea that has taken form with the aim of saving Lake Chad. It first emerged 30 years ago as the Italian-led Transaqua project to transfer water from the northern tributaries of the Congo River through the Central African Republic via a gigantic 2,400-kilometre canal.

This canal is now being promoted vigorously by the Lake Chad Basin Commission (LCBC), which comprises Cameroon, Chad, Niger, Nigeria and the Central African Republic. CIMA+, one of Canada's largest engineering companies, was hired in 2009 by the LCBC to prepare a feasibility study for the water transfer project.[11] In addition to halting the shrinkage of Lake Chad, the Commission's objectives are: 1) to build a multipurpose dam on the Ubangi River to generate hydropower for Bangui and areas in the two Congos; 2) to stimulate navigation between the two basins; and 3) to support economic activities such as agriculture, fishing and livestock breeding.

On the diplomatic front, agreements have been signed between the members of the Commission and by the governments in Brazzaville and Kinshasa. But the project is still on hold. Funding is inadequate and environmental impact assessments have indicated high environmental costs such as the loss of hydroelectricity potential, navigation problems, even more pressure on fish stocks and the introduction of exotic species. There are also worries about high evaporation rates, which could jeopardise the whole idea. International pressure on Congo and the high economic stakes involved, however, could convince Congolese elites, someday, to allow the scheme to move ahead.

Hydroelectricity

Congo has 13 per cent of the Earth's hydropower potential. This is one of the country's greatest assets. The development of this clean and renewable energy could have positive consequences for local communities and global environmental sustainability. It could foster rapid national economic growth and progress in many African countries. In the medium or long term, it could help the country obtain carbon credit funding. Congo has tremendous solar power potential too – but that is also still underexploited. The sector, nevertheless, is trapped in contradiction: so much potential, so little power. The Congo has a hydroelectric potential of 100,000 megawatts but only 2,500 are harnessed and only 1,600 are operational. Because only an estimated 9 per cent of the Congolese population is served by the national energy grid (run by the Société Nationale d'Électricité or SNEL), people have no alternative but to cook with charcoal, the production of which is a main driver of deforestation and therefore global climate change.[12]

Energy scarcity is also an overwhelming handicap to industrial productivity. Katanga's formal mining business – the mainstay of the Congolese formal economy – is dependent on electricity. Nevertheless, it simply does not have enough power to function efficiently today. When the Ministers of Mines and Finance signed a directive banning the export of unprocessed copper and cobalt in April 2013, Katanga Governor Moïse Katumbi refused to enforce the rule, citing the lack of electricity as the reason for this.[13] The private sector identifies electricity scarcity as a greater obstacle to doing business in Congo than access to finance, political instability or even corruption.[14] Nearly 60 per cent of companies therefore own or share a diesel-run generator.[15] Energy scarcity also has dire public health repercussions.

While Congo's hydropower is still largely untapped, new electricity needs on the African continent and technological innovation are indications of a promising future for the sector. As revealed in Figure 4.2 and Table 4.2, there are an estimated 766 waterfall sites.[16] Each one has at least a 500-kilowatt potential but most have much more.[17] The map also indicates a great divergence in the number of sites and the total amount of hydropower potential by province. Bas-Congo, for example, has only 24 sites but a huge 64,000-megawatt potential. By contrast, Maniema has 140 sites – more than any other province – but a relatively low total hydropower potential of 458 megawatts.

Figure 4.2 Hydroelectric power potential in the DRC

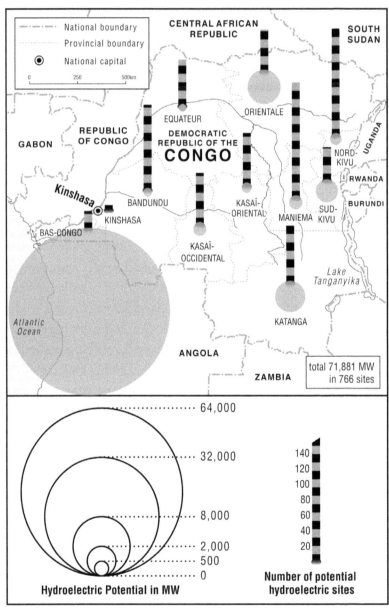

Source: République Démocratique du Congo and Ministère des Ressources Hydrauliques et Électricité (2014).

Table 4.2 Hydroelectric power potential in the DRC

Province	Megawatts	Sites
Kinshasa	n/a	8
Bandundu	172	114
Bas-Congo	64,000	24
Equateur	122	58
Kasaï-Occidental	433	64
Kasaï-Oriental	252	65
Katanga	2,231	70
Maniema	458	140
North Kivu	332	130
Orientale	2,684	52
South Kivu	1,197	41
Total	71,881	766

Source: République Démocratique du Congo and Ministère des Ressources Hydrauliques et Électricité (2014).

The abundant small hydropower opportunities (between 1 and 20 megawatts) are those that could meaningfully boost local development by providing electricity for agricultural transformation, industry, small-scale mining and skilled crafts. These are typically run-of-the-river schemes that do not create large reservoirs so they generally tend to have limited environmental impacts compared with conventional and larger hydroelectric installations. At another level, small generators on Congo's streams could easily provide remote communities with enough electricity for lighting, charging mobile phones, operating a sewing machine or mill, or listening to a radio. Pico hydro, a term used for hydroelectric power generation of less than 5 kilowatts, is a good example of locally appropriate technology. The turbine and pipe installations are low-tech, relatively cheap and easily maintained.

Small-scale development projects (rural healthcare clinics, food production and transformation initiatives or church associations, for example) are increasingly investing in their own energy-producing installations. People in urban environments prefer petrol-run generators to replace or supplement the national grid. Small 5-kilowatt generators, such as those typically used by shopkeepers in towns, tend to run on petrol whereas larger generators usually run on diesel, or, in some cases, heavy-duty fuel oil. Rural communities, however, do not have access to petrol or diesel fuel, and so pico hydro is a more attractive alternative for them.

During the colonial period, many private companies built their own dams to generate power because their needs preceded the creation of a national grid. Today, the country has some old or refurbished hydroelectric production plants, including Inga I and II and Zongo I in Bas-Congo, Tshopo in Orientale, Mobayi in Equateur, Bendera, Nseke and Nzilo in Katanga, Tshiala-Lubilash in Kasaï-Oriental and Ruzizi I and II in South Kivu. Others are under construction: Zongo II in Bas-Congo (funded by China), and Kakobola in Bandundu and Grand Katende in Kasaï-Occidental (both funded by India). The Virunga National Park recently built a hydroelectric plant at Mutwanga and is constructing one on the Rutshuru River at Matebe (funded by the Howard Buffett Foundation). Others are planned for the near future, such as Ruzizi III in South Kivu. Their capacity is important for specifically targeted users – and this is a significant development improvement – but they are too few and far between to satisfy the macro-level needs of households and industries.

The government has committed to electrifying rural areas, in part because electricity is the first thing villagers ask for from the state. The setting up of the National Agency for Rural Energy Services (Agence Nationale des Services Énergétiques Ruraux or ANSER) is a step in this direction. Local politicians and elites derive electoral advantages from this type of initiative because, once villages are equipped with even a small dam and a distribution network, they are likely to be elected or re-elected. The government is also campaigning to find foreign investors for micro hydroelectric installations. In an effort to attract investors, it has also liberalised the national power sector, allowing new actors to generate, distribute and sell electricity. In a similar vein, the national electricity board (SNEL), which was a state-run monopoly until recently, has become a limited company – but with the state as sole owner.

The Inga Dam complex in Bas-Congo is the country's hydro-power jewel in the crown. The African Union promotes it as a priority public–private initiative that could contribute to reducing sub-Saharan Africa's energy deficit. As the DRC enjoys near total sovereignty over the Congo River, conflicts such as those between Ethiopia and Egypt over dam construction and its impact on the Nile do not exist – although they could if water is diverted towards the Lake Chad Basin. Two dams already exist: Inga I (which appeared on Mobutu's 5 Zaire banknote), built in 1972 with a capacity of 351 megawatts, and Inga II, built in 1982 with a 1,424-megawatt capacity. These dams, however, produce only a fraction of their potential. Output is low because of lack of maintenance (a political and economic choice) and heavy silting (an ecological problem). Half of the turbines are out of service.

Inga III and Grand Inga, both in the project stage, are two additional sites that could boost Inga's hydroelectric potential to a staggering 44,000 megawatts. Three consortia are candidates in the selection process to develop Inga III: Sinohydro and China Three Gorges Corporation from China; Actividades de Construcción y Servicios (ACS), Eurofinsa and AEE from Spain; and the Daewoo–Posco–SNC Lavalin consortium from Korea and Canada. The American law firm Orrick, Herrington & Sutcliffe, the investment bank Lazard and Tractebel Engineering, the engineering consultancy of GDF Suez, have teamed up to assist the Congolese government on the management and implementation of the project.[18] The involvement of these actors proves that interest in Inga extends well beyond the realm of the Congolese authorities – who, as a consequence, are dependent upon outside factors over which they have little control.

In comparison, China's Three Gorges hydroelectric dam on the Yangtze River, currently the world's largest, generates 22,500 megawatts. The Itaipu Dam between Brazil and Paraguay on the Paraná River produces 14,000 megawatts. When completed in 2017, the Grand Ethiopian Renaissance Dam will be the largest in Africa with an output of 6,000 megawatts. In other words, Inga dwarfs all other hydroelectric sites the world over. Electricity produced by Inga is also estimated to be the cheapest in the world per kilowatt-hour. In addition, and largely because of the high natural water flow, social and environment impact assessments indicate that 'the positive impacts outweigh the negative impacts'.[19]

Nevertheless, the challenges to moving ahead with the Inga III and Grand Inga projects are proportionally daunting. François Misser has studied Inga meticulously over the past few years and describes the scheme as a 'saga'.[20] In a previous in-depth study, Jean-Claude Willame described it as an 'epic'.[21] Both terms are apposite because Inga's story is long, involved and complicated, with multiple actors and high stakes, and whose outcome remains uncertain. One major obstacle is cost, which is estimated at between $50 billion and $80 billion.[22] The World Bank and African Development Bank expressed firm interest in investing in the project but President Obama recently signed the 2014 Consolidated Appropriation Act. The result of efficient lobbying by a California-based non-governmental organisation (NGO), International Rivers, this Act bans any US funding going into large dam projects, even via lending agencies such as the World Bank, the International Monetary Fund or the African Development Bank.[23] (International Rivers is opposed to large dams because of their potential social and environmental threats.) This has created some confusion amongst donors and in the field because engineers have already been recruited and are working on construction design, financial planning and geological studies.[24] Confirming that Inga is indeed an ongoing saga, funding is now, once again, on hold.

This is not the only setback. The Australian mining giant BHP Billiton was interested in investing in Inga III to fuel a proposed aluminium smelter in Bas-Congo but bowed out due to soaring costs, a drop in aluminium prices on the international market and insufficient additional private investment commitments.[25] South Africa, which badly needs new sources of electricity to run its mines, has been heavily involved in negotiations too, but, again, nothing has materialised yet. In fact, reports have circulated that Russia will provide up to eight nuclear reactors to South Africa by 2023 at an estimated cost of $50 billion.[26] If the deal goes through, South Africa will be less interested in investing in Inga.

Producing hydroelectric power from large dams is both a challenge and an opportunity. So is transporting energy from a dam to end users, as is selling it, which is often the weak link in electricity schemes. An electricity highway map has been drawn up, starting at Inga. It is theoretical and optimistic but does reflect a realistic forecast of the continent's mid-term energy needs. Destinations are: 1) South Africa via Angola, Namibia and Botswana; 2) South Africa via Zambia and Zimbabwe; 3) Egypt via the Republic of Congo, Central African Republic and Sudan; 4) Nigeria via the Republic of Congo, Gabon and Cameroon; and 5) Kenya via Zambia and Tanzania. High-tension power transmission is not new to Congo and the international engineering know-how exists. One of Mobutu's grandiose technological projects, supported by his Western – mainly American – backers, was the construction of a 1,700-kilometre high-voltage line extending from Inga to Kolwezi in the mineral-rich Katanga province.[27] Completed in 1982 at a cost of around $1 billion, it was the longest high-voltage direct-current line in the world until 2010, when the Chinese built a link from the Xiangjiaba Dam to Shanghai.

Inga epitomises Congo's vulnerability in a globalised economic system in which the Congolese are relatively powerless to take charge of their own hydroelectric potential. Global issues including the drop in aluminium prices, the Russia–South Africa deal for the supply of nuclear reactors and NGO lobbying against large dams have a direct impact on national macroeconomic planning and priorities. Global warming, changing rainfall patterns and the water transfer project could alter the flow of the Congo River and consequently affect production estimates. Protecting long-distance transmission cables against terrorist attacks is another worry; a precedent for this exists because rebel groups fighting against President Mobutu previously succeeded in disrupting the Inga–Kolwezi line.

Some opponents of Inga argue that the work would create a new spiral of indebtedness that the country can ill afford. Another debate around Inga pertains to users and benefits. Today, high-tension cables pass over villages that are not connected to the grid and remain in the dark. Dispatching electricity all over Africa without ensuring that ordinary Congolese are connected raises serious ethical questions of legitimacy. Yet another highly politicised debate relates to strategic choices concerning centralised or decentralised hydropower. Should the government and inter-national partners promote regional installations to support the stalled decentralisation process, or should they focus on the mega Inga project? Although the two are not mutually exclusive and it would make sense to pursue both options simultaneously, this priority policy issue remains unresolved. The government is well aware of the need to make decisions and has partially addressed these issues in a strategic document – at least on paper.[28]

Transportation

Congo is greatly dependent on its river and lake network for the transportation of goods and people. Investment in the development and management of river and port infrastructure, as well as safe ships, is therefore a prerequisite for the improved mobility of both. Motorised canoes, barges and heavily laden wooden boats (which have gradually replaced the colonial steamboat) relentlessly ply the waters. These waterways are just as important as agricultural feeder roads for getting produce to markets. They provide – in many cases – the most efficient return in terms of tonnage of goods transported per kilometre. Concrete examples include floating tropical tree logs down the Congo River from Equateur and Orientale provinces assisted by tugboats, travelling by passenger ferry between Goma and Bukavu on Lake Kivu, and shipping bags of corn and cassava in wooden boats from the Kasaï and Kwilu rivers of Bandundu to feed Kinshasa. Men paddling dugout canoes full of smoked fish or bushmeat, along with their families, maintain an age-old and omnipresent transportation practice. The dugout canoe continues to serve vital livelihood needs.

While there is clearly a need for improved rail and road infrastructure in many parts of the country (for mineral exports from Katanga, for example), ecological constraints make river transport the logical option elsewhere, notably throughout the immense floodplains of the central basin. Nevertheless, there is an overwhelming obstacle to commercial transportation along the Congo River: the succession of 32 cataracts between Kinshasa and Matadi makes shipping between the coast and the capital impossible. This significantly increases the costs of most imports and exports (especially timber). The railway between Kinshasa and Matadi, built in the late 1880s, is expensive, inefficient and unreliable. As a result, development planners are giving serious consideration to building a road-and-rail bridge between Kinshasa and Brazzaville (the two closest capital cities in the world) in order to connect Kinshasa to the Congo–Ocean railway, an existing rail line that links Brazzaville to the Atlantic deep-water port at Pointe-Noire. Feasibility studies have also been carried out to examine the possibility of building a canal to circumvent the cataracts and thus make river traffic between Kinshasa and the Atlantic possible.[29] Development planners do not seem to take this option seriously, however, because it is largely viewed as a pipe dream.

The river network is managed by the state-owned agency Régie des Voies Fluviales (RVF). Its responsibilities include marking navigation routes (which vary according to the season), controlling cargo weights and passenger capacity, monitoring boat construction norms and making sure that private port facilities comply with national rules and regulations. But the RVF does not have the capacity to respect its mandate, which accounts for the poor security situation on Congo's waters. Reports of boats capsizing and people drowning are regular news items in the Congolese media. Even the Transportation Minister himself, Justin Kalumba, complained about these dangers and the 'disorderly' nature of river transport.[30] Administrative hassles and predation by state agents taking advantage of traders on the river network are another aspect of this disorder.[31] The Régie des Voies Maritimes (RVM) is a sister agency of the RVF and is responsible for the 148-kilometre maritime reach and for managing the ports at Boma, Matadi and Banana. The Société Commerciale des Transports et des Ports (known as the Office National des Transports until 2011) manages these ports on behalf of the RVM. Other important ports include those at Kinshasa, Kalemie (on Lake Tanganyika) and Ilebo (on the Kasai River near its junction with the Sankuru River). Ilebo is an important transportation hub because it has rail connections with Kananga and Lubumbashi. Their potential but poor management and inadequate funding are the common denominators of these port facilities.

Drinking water, sanitation and energy

Another incredible blue-gold paradox relates to drinking water – which has become a real social crisis. Statistics are sketchy, but the best sources suggest that only 26 per cent, or just one Congolese in four, has access to safe drinking water: one in three in urban areas but only one in six among rural communities.[32] This puts Congo well below the sub-Saharan average of 61 per cent.[33] Average consumption per capita is also comparatively low, in part because only nine Congolese cities have functioning water distribution networks.[34] How can so many people living in a country with so much water be thirsty? The challenge of improving the situation involves a combination of political, demographic and economic factors. Water scarcity can be a result of two mechanisms: physical water scarcity and economic water scarcity. The first is caused by inadequate natural water resources to supply a region's demand; the second is a result of poor management of sufficient water resources. In the case of the DRC, scarcity clearly results from poor management. As with the electricity sector, the government plans to liberalise the water sector and to privatise the delivery of some of its services.

Water scarcity defines people's lives, putting a conspicuous strain on their well-being, health and hygiene, finances, family relations and time management. For elderly urban Congolese, running water is little more than a memory, a remnant of the colonial past. The struggle to find water for drinking, cooking and washing is paramount in the daily trials confronting women and young girls – even though men are increasingly participating in water procurement chores. The more vulnerable the community, the higher the price they tend to pay for water in terms of purchase price (water from a neighbourhood standpipe costs more than tap water), transportation expenses, physical effort and time loss.

Regideso is the state agency officially mandated to provide water treatment and distribution in urban areas across the country, while the Service National de l'Hydraulique Rurale was set up in 1983 to serve rural areas. Roughly half of Kinshasa's population of 10 million has access to Regideso infrastructure.[35] This means that 5 million people living in the nation's capital do not – especially those living in the city's poor and crowded districts such as Masina and Kimbanseke or in those far from the colonial city centre, such as Maluku. A 2001 study reported that 2 million *Kinois* did not have access to the Regideso network.[36] So, despite efforts to increase water availability, 3 million more *Kinois* are facing a water deficit today, largely due to the city's relentless population boom. Demographic growth far exceeds any increase in the potable water supply.

In the diamond-rich city of Mbuji-Mayi (approximately 1.5 million inhabitants), the number of people connected to public water plummeted between 2002 and 2012, going from 18,000 to

3,000. The paradox is compounded here by the fact that the city has clean underground spring water but Regideso does not have the electricity needed to pump it into the network. Goma and Bukavu, as well as most other Congolese cities, are in the same situation, and water scarcity leads to regular outbreaks of cholera, dysentery and other diseases. Typhoid, which is transmitted through food or water contaminated with the excrement of an infected person, is a recurrent problem: 25 people died during a typhoid outbreak in Kasaï-Oriental in 2014, for example.[37]

The case of water consumption at the University of Kinshasa may appear to be anecdotal but it provides thought-provoking insight into broader patterns throughout the country.[38] The university was established in 1954 to accommodate a student population of 5,000. Today, there are 30,000 students. At peak moments during the week, with workers, traders, shop-keepers and other service providers, there are up to 40,000 people on campus. Ninety-five per cent of residents complain of water scarcity, stating that water runs out of the tap only 5 per cent of the time, and in dribbles at best. It can take hours to fill a bucket. There is an average of eight women per dormitory room and four men in rooms that were built for single occupancy. But access to water is only half the struggle; there is also the problem of sanitation and the management of kitchen and human waste. There were seven toilets for 7,000 dormitory residents in 2001.[39] Some latrines have been built since then, but 'humanly unacceptable and unfortunate' conditions remain the norm.[40] A project aimed at reducing water scarcity on campus is being considered. Cost estimates for replacing and refurbishing piping and plumbing exceed those for drilling, storing and pumping water into the university buildings.

There is a direct causal relationship between water-related illness and energy scarcity. Water stored in cisterns and plastic jugs contaminates easily and, in many cases, a contaminated jug is more of a risk than the water itself. To eliminate bacteria, it is recommended that water be boiled for at least 30 minutes and then filtered before drinking, but to boil or not to boil water raises a Cornelian dilemma. Most urban families use charcoal as their primary source of cooking fuel but access to charcoal is just as difficult as access to water. Mothers have to make strategic choices about how to use it. They tend to prefer using it to cook food rather than to boil water. Despite the prevalence of water-borne intestinal diseases, boiling water is widely perceived as a poor use of scarce charcoal. An alternative to boiling water is adding chlorine or tincture of iodine tablets, but few people do this. They are not used to doing so, do not have money to buy these products, and do not like the taste. Most importantly, they are afraid of being poisoned.[41]

Water scarcity, inadequate sanitation infrastructure and poor health are also directly linked, especially in urban and peri-urban areas. The country's urban rivers in most provinces are open sewers, polluted by wastewater, household trash, plastics of all sorts, garbage and excrement from humans and domestic animals. Phosphates found in washing detergents (in addition to bathing, people wash their clothes in the rivers) and chemicals used for urban agriculture along their banks contaminate these rivers. Although people know that these activities pollute, they say they have no alternative. Mining industry practices and the lack of proper enforcement of existing regulations are also threats. Many water tables and much surface water in Katanga, for example, are lethal habitats, contaminated with cadmium, lead, mercury and copper.

Water scarcity is a poignant example of the multidimensional crisis that the vast majority of Congolese live through every day – and one that reinforces the argument for integrating sector mana-gement policies, in this case energy in particular. The Congolese government plays an oversight role but does little to improve the state of the drinking water sector itself. International partners have taken up this challenge and are responsible for 95 per cent of related investments, spending approximately $62 million per annum in recent years.[42] These efforts are meaningful but fall far short of redressing a situation that has deteriorated over decades of neglect. There are two main aid strategies. One is the rehabilitation of Regideso infrastructure and the expansion of its network. The second is more innovative and community-based. It entails setting up small-scale autonomous production and distribution networks that include borehole drilling, pumping stations, storage tanks and distribution fountains. Despite the fact that users pay for water directly at the fountain, they appear to have appropriated this approach because they are involved in its management and because it offers them a viable alternative to the discredited public system.[43]

Fishing and fish farming

While the main focus of this book is on the present and future potential of Congo's natural resources, this section on fishing presents an example of lost – and probably irretrievable – potential. The Belgians, who were once proud to say that they could drive their Volkswagen Beetles from Stanleyville to Leopoldville in three days, also claimed that there were so many fish in Congo's waters that they died of old age. If this were ever true, it certainly is not today. The practice of catching large fish with harpoons, observed by Robert Harms in the late 1970s,[44] has died out too. Fish capture is increasingly challenging. Average fish size is smaller and catch volumes are diminishing. Waters are overfished, poorly managed and regulated, and increasingly polluted.

There are an estimated 1,782 species of aquatic invertebrates and around 1,000 fish in the DRC.[45] Although official reports still tend to cite outdated data – referring to an annual catch potential of 707,000 tonnes[46] – informed opinion is that this is a gross exaggeration.[47] In 1984, when the country's population was 30.5 million, the catch was estimated at 150,000 tonnes per year.[48] It is currently around 200,000 tonnes, representing an unambiguous decrease in catch per capita given the growth in the population.[49] In all types of waters – fresh, brackish and ocean – fish stocks are under threat. Fishing techniques and practices are the major culprits.

People no longer respect spawning seasons and now use fine-mesh nets (such as the mosquito nets distributed for free by public health NGOs), which are serious impediments to regeneration. Although some fish species mature quickly and spawn more than once a year, others do not reach reproduction for at least a few years.

Most communities that live near water fish, in addition to carrying out other subsistence activities such as farming and hunting. There are numerous techniques and practices with different kinds of paraphernalia, but the basic equipment is a dugout canoe and a net. As most Congolese live near water, this translates into hundreds of thousands of occasional or artisanal fisherman and fisherwomen, which is far too many people harvesting from a vulnerable fish base. The predicament it represents, however, is understandable, because present needs are perceived as having precedence over future well-being. Eating fish is culturally engrained and is a main source of sustenance for tens of millions of Congolese. Also, the money earned from selling surpluses is a helpful supplement to family incomes. Popular perceptions about sustainability are problematic. When asked if they thought that stocks could disappear in Lake Mai-Ndombe, a group of adult fishermen responded that it was unimaginable because of the quantity of sand around the lake. Whether they believed it or not, they said that the grains of sand were eggs and grew into fish.[50]

There is a link between reliance on fish for protein and the decreasing availability of bushmeat. Habitat loss and commercial hunting have reduced the volume of wild animals that people also rely on for sustenance. There is also a link between fishing and deforestation – not necessarily in all areas, but certainly in some key biodiversity hotspots. Smoking fish is an age-old practice but one that requires large quantities of wood. Fishing communities on Lake Edward, for example, are responsible for unsustainable deforestation in the Virunga National Park, threatening wildlife habitat.[51]

Once a relatively important formal economic activity, especially in the Great Lakes Region, industrial fishing is practically non-existent today. Fishing trawlers were poorly maintained after independence, broke down and were not replaced, especially after sweeping nationalisations in 1974. There were also problems of getting spare parts and fuel. The sector was run largely by Greek migrants, but once their companies were nationalised they either left the country or engaged in other activities. Lack of energy makes refrigeration nearly impossible and serious transportation deficiencies mean that getting fresh fish to markets is difficult. As with other Congolese foods that could be produced locally, it is often cheaper to import them, which explains the prevalence in the Congolese diet of low-quality frozen horse mackerel (*mpiodi*, nicknamed *thompson*) from the Namibian coasts and Norwegian salt cod (*makayabu*). Dried and smoked fish is also imported from Lake Victoria. A national fishing and fish-farming strategy will need to find alternatives to the import of poor-quality products while striking a balance between the expectations of consumers and the delivery capacity of producers.

While the possibility of feeding the Congolese population from fishing is certainly remote and probably lost, fish farming still has the potential to be a highly worthwhile development option. There is an international boom in fish farming in much of Africa, boosted by the sector's growth in Asia. This is a result of two factors: the increase in fish farming know-how and the depletion of natural fish stocks in the wild. Worldwide, nearly half of all fish for human consumption now comes from farms: 47 per cent in 2010 compared with 9 per cent in 1980.[52] There are more tonnes of fish produced in fish farms today than beef from ranches – this represents a major shift in food production.[53]

Fish farming in Congo enjoyed a spectacular past. It was introduced in Katanga in 1946 as a subsistence strategy: the expanding number of people working in the copper mines needed to be fed. This was the first African experience with the idea. By 1960, there were 122,000 ponds belonging to 15,000 farmers, raising tilapia.[54] In the immediate post-independence years, however, fish farming came to a complete standstill. These ponds, once teeming with fish for food, are now empty.

Fish farming is not a particularly complex enterprise. It does, however, depend upon the right blend of biological, economic and engineering knowledge in addition to a specific support structure. Intensive or semi-intensive hatcheries are necessary to produce fry and manage fingerlings – and these require a constant source of electricity. Specialised feed mills need to be maintained because the volume and quality of the fish depend on the quality of feed. Farmers need coaching in how to maintain their ponds and stock, to avoid the degeneration of strains of cultivated species, to get the right balance of fish densities per cubic metre of water, and to understand appropriate drainage techniques. This set of conditions helps explain the rapid decline of fish farming after independence and also points to what needs to be done now to redress the situation. The fundamental prerequisites include significant financial investment, training, infrastructure and political will. The shift from a subsistence model to a national food production strategy is another major policy priority.

International partners – both public and private – are aware of the potential of fish farming in the DRC and are preparing development strategies. Belgian Technical Cooperation, for example, has invested in an important artisanal fisheries and aquaculture project in Katanga.[55] A group of private sector entrepreneurs in and around Kinshasa has formed the Groupement Agro-Piscicole de Kinshasa to improve their production and commercialisation practices. The government is also working with well-respected international partners such as the African, Caribbean and Pacific Group of States on the European Union ACP FISH II (EU) programme, which has been supporting the Ministry of Agriculture and Livestock to prepare a national policy for fisheries and aquaculture.[56] This ministry has also received the support of the Food and Agriculture Organization of the United Nations to prepare a new law for fisheries and aquaculture (*Code de Pêche et d'Aquaculture*) and to help draw up an aquaculture development plan. Objectives of the law include, most notably, improving the efficiency of production systems, intensification, market support and improving management through training and professionalization. The parliamentary process to have these documents approved is ongoing. The policy and institutional framework is therefore evolving constructively, but the challenges of funding and implementation are still unresolved.[57]

Water governance

Congo's legal and institutional framework cannot cope with the diversity of water-related priorities, and, although it is in the process of being updated, it is ill adapted to meet current social, economic and industrial needs. There is such a plethora of legal codes, decrees, by-laws, rules and regulations (some dating from the colonial period) that no one has a clear overview of how to interpret or apply them.[58] Table 4.3 reveals how intricate the institutional framework is today: six different ministries are mandated with sometimes distinct, sometimes overlapping water management responsibilities. This makes decision making about budgets, responsibilities, international partnerships, ecological concerns and public health extremely cumbersome. With so many actors involved, no one really accepts ownership of or responsibility for water governance.

This institutional complexity helps account for the fact that the DRC does not have a national water policy. The government does not have a vision of what it expects water governance to look like in the coming years. This is a problem that some other sectors suffer from too. There is no framework law or single ministry mandated with water management oversight. There are, however, indications that the government is trying to tackle these deficiencies. A Water Code was drafted in 2010 with German development assistance. It sets out a comprehensive structure for sustainable water management and has been discussed in parliament, but approval is still pending. Its guiding principles are: 1) users pay for water; 2) polluters pay for degradation;

Table 4.3 Water sector institutions and their roles

Institution	Role in water management
Ministry of Environment and Sustainable Development	Supervisory authority over the Institut Congolais pour la Conservation de la Nature for conservation of aquatic eco-systems and development of watershed management plans
	Facilitating international and regional water cooperation
Ministry of Hydraulic Resources and Energy (formerly Ministry of Energy)	Supervisory authority over Régie des Distributions d'Eau for urban drinking water supply
	Supervisory authority over Société Nationale d'Électricité for hydropower
	Issuing permits for hydropower plant construction
Ministry of Rural Development	Development of rural and peri-urban drinking water supply
	Supervisory authority over Service National d'Hydraulique Rurale
Ministry of Public Health	Control of drinking water quality
Ministry of Transportation	Supervisory authority over RVF for river transport
	Supervisory authority over RVM for river transport
	Supervisory authority over Agence Nationale de Météorologie et Télédétection par Satellite for meteorological data collection
Ministry of Planning	Supervisory authority over the Comité National d'Action de l'Eau et de l'Assainissement
	Inter-ministerial and interdepartmental coordination
	Focal point for international development partners

Source: Research synthesis based mainly on UNEP (2011a).

3) acceptance of an integrated use approach; 4) integration of pre-cautionary risk management strategies; 5) decentralised rights and responsibilities in harmony with the Constitution; 6) stakeholder participation; and 7) transborder cooperation.[59]

Although they have limited impact, regional water governance initiatives also exist. For example, evidence of the effects of climate variability and change on water resources provided the impetus to set up the International Commission of the Congo–Ubangi–Sangha Basin (CICOS) in 1999. Cameroon, the Central African Republic, the DRC and the Republic of Congo established CICOS to improve water management cooperation.

The accidental or deliberate introduction of exotic species into Congo's waters is a problem that can be countered only by improved governance, monitoring and scientific expertise. Experiences in other African countries need to be taken into account: for example, the Nile perch was released into Lake Victoria in the 1950s, but because it is such a dominant predator, it has significantly altered the lake's ecosystem in the last few decades. Water hyacinth is already a concern on Congo's rivers because it hampers navigation in some areas and disrupts the functioning of hydroelectric turbines.

The ill-adapted institutional framework and the great diversity of Congo's water resources point to a number of rather troublesome questions. Should water be treated as a commodity? If so, to whom does it belong? Can the often conflicting needs of all stakeholders be reconciled? Is the institutional framework appropriate? Do Congolese civil servants and professionals have the vision and skills to improve water management? Can international partnerships help? The obvious responses to these questions do not allow for optimism. The immensity of Congo's water resources is proportional to the governance challenges in managing them and using them for development.

Conclusion: integrating water management strategies

Is an integrated water management strategy possible? Perhaps someday, but establishing such an approach faces a double challenge in Congo today. Firstly, there is the water itself. It is extremely difficult to integrate issues such as hydropower, river navigation, drinking water and sanitation, and fish stock management in one overarching policy framework. The integrated water resources management approach – adopted by development agencies, NGOs and technical experts – is internationally accepted best practice based on the assumption that a more holistic vision is essential.

Because water issues cannot be considered in isolation, they argue, fragmented strategies are no longer viable.[60]

While this philosophy makes some sense for the Congo, it is difficult to conceptualise and implement because the country's water resources are so diverse, so subject to unsustainable use and so neglected by the Congolese government and development agencies. This challenge is exacerbated by the frequently conflictual involvement of a host of stakeholders. Moreover, actions tend to be fragmented and based on a vertical project approach. While improved water governance will gradually need to follow an integrated approach, this is idealistic for the time being. Many important enabling conditions need to be established first. Capacity building, public and private financial investment, vision and government commitment in the specific water subsectors are prerequisites for a viable integrated approach.

Secondly, there is the challenge of establishing a policy framework that extends beyond the water sector itself and connects with other priority sectors. This chapter has discussed how deforestation is a direct result of underexploited hydropower and how industrial mining is restricted by energy scarcity. It has shown how the national water board is hobbled by energy shortages too: even though water may be available and abundant, it requires energy to get it into the water distribution system. Similarly, without refrigeration, fish production will not be able to improve households' food security.

This chapter has also focused on the international dimension of Congo's water resources, emphasising the inability of Congolese decision makers to exercise full sovereignty over the country's lakes and rivers. Transborder water disputes over oilfields or fishing rights are a threat to regional diplomacy, for example, and the drop in international aluminium prices and then a political decision in Washington DC threw funding decisions for Inga into disarray. Improved management of Congo's water resources is therefore contingent upon international factors as well as on national forestry, agricultural and energy issues. Parallels can be drawn between the potential of water and other resources: water could be a driver of economic and social development and could play an important ecological role, but policies that integrate sectors, and institutional frameworks, need to evolve before this will happen.

Chapter 5

OIL: PLENTY FOR SOME, NOTHING FOR MOST

Introduction

Congo has oil too – in addition to all of its other natural wealth. Black gold has the potential to help Congo develop but it could also be a new resource curse. Oil production is more than likely to be an environmental calamity, even though it will probably be many years before it increases significantly. Lack of transparency, controversy, shady 'flipping' deals and high economic stakes haunt the Congolese oil business in the same way they do mining. The gap between oil potential and oil production is wide, as it is for the other resources analysed in this book. One of the very few Congolese hydrocarbon geologists has described the oil sector as 'lethargic', and accounts for this sluggishness by the imbalanced emphasis on mining[1] – a typical Dutch disease problem. Other global and national political economy factors also sustain the relative lack of investment in the sector. Up until recently, when the Asian need for oil expanded, more accessible sources were able to cover global demands. Investors require strong incentives to pump from landlocked areas – a problem that Gulf of Guinea producers did not face. Exploration and pumping oil are relatively easy. Getting that oil to a port, however, is far more challenging.

There is no easy bonanza for oil investors in Congo today. Boosting production will require political accommodation, reduced tension in diplomatic relations with Angola and Uganda, major infrastructure development, investment stability and managerial vision. It is also contingent upon strong technical expertise and the support of competent civil servants. Improved governance is another recurrent prerequisite. 'Good oil governance requires transparency, political leadership, and collective action from below,' maintains Douglas Yates.[2] Can Congo meet these requirements, given the present governance environment? At present, the sector is poorly organised and run from the presidency – not the relevant ministry. In addition to global constraints and opportunities, its development depends largely on the motivation of President Kabila, his political allies and his business cronies, such as Dan Gertler.

Unlike all of the other environmental sectors presented in this volume, where ordinary Congolese derive some direct or indirect benefits, oil is essentially an enclave economy. Congo's oil sector is not unlike that of other African countries, such as Angola, where 'there are minimal linkages to the rest of the economy'.[3] Oil production is a highly capital-intensive economic activity with limited employment opportunities and little trickle-down through shared benefits. The current situation in Congo confirms James Ferguson's analysis of African oil production in general as being a process of 'extractive enclaving'.[4] In a study on new African oil producers – a category in which the DRC could be considered – Celeste Hicks draws attention to the seemingly unavoidable problem of oil's limited contribution to national macroeconomic development.[5]

Congo has been in the news for negative reasons in recent years: war in the Kivus, sexual violence against women and the illegal trade of conflict minerals. Oil exploration in Africa's oldest national park is the latest addition to this list of problems. When I first started researching this chapter, a geologist colleague warned me: 'Congo's industrial mining sector is rotten, but it is like Sunday school compared to the cut-throat oil business.'[6] His observation was useful in preparing me for the arcane nature of this emerging geo-strategic sector in Congo. Total's pressure on François Hollande to attend the *Sommet de la Francophonie* in Kinshasa in 2012 is a good example of the clout of oil companies in Africa. The French president was reluctant to attend the summit because of widely accepted accusations of electoral fraud orchestrated by Kabila's camp the year before.[7] The oil giant, however, made it clear to him that boycotting the summit would not be good for French oil politics in the region.[8]

This chapter presents an overview of the main opportunities and challenges relating to the political economy of Congo's oil sector. Although oil is the country's third most important export earner, only a few researchers have attempted an examination of reserves and production or the way in which oil shapes national policies and regional relations. As it is a relatively new extractive activity, there is not much historical analysis to build upon. The analysis here can therefore be considered as an early tracking exercise that brings together scattered writings, some in English but most in French. Oil has become big business in the DRC and the subject of major deal making – more often than not by dubious partners. It is shrouded in secrecy and controlled directly by the presidency. The chapter presents some basic background to the sector and continues with a presentation of the regulatory framework. The conflict-prone nature of regional politics is analysed in the following section, while the fourth part focuses on the controversies surrounding oil exploration in the Virunga National Park. It concludes by arguing that, despite the obstacles, the sector will continue to grow, but as an enclave economy with few immediate development benefits.

Potential untapped

Congo's petroleum potential, although promising, remains largely unexplored and unknown.[9] Its geography is fragmented. Current production takes place solely onshore and offshore along the Atlantic coast in the Bas-Congo province. Exploration is ongoing in the Western Rift Valley, where concessions have been awarded. Unsubstantiated and wildly optimistic rumours are circulating about reserves in the central basin. Some claim that there could be even more oil there than in Saudi Arabia![10] Lake Tanganyika is also suspected of having oil but neither Congo nor Zambia has started exploration; however, Burundi and Tanzania have issued exploration licences there.[11] There are also significant reserves of methane gas in Lake Kivu, which straddles the border between Congo and Rwanda. Rwanda has initiated some small-scale projects to convert gas into electricity, mainly one to power a brewery. The technology to extract gas from Lake Kivu is accessible, as is proved by the Rwandan projects, and the gas could be distributed through low-cost pipeline networks to cities such as Goma and Bukavu. Congolese decision makers, however, have been disinclined to explore this potential so far. Security concerns are the obvious reason, but Kivu's geographical and political distance from Kinshasa is an equally powerful explanation for foot-dragging.

Oil exploration and production are relatively new to the Congo. Petrofina, which has merged and mutated over the past century, was the first company to be involved in the oil distribution sector in Congo. It was originally created in 1911 to supply imported fuel to the Matadi–Leopoldville railway.[12] Exploration began in the late colonial period but production did not start until 1976, initiated by Chevron. Oil production over the past decade has hovered at around 25,000 barrels per day, a drop from 30,000 barrels per day in the mid-1990s. This puts the DRC in the category of minor oil-producing countries.

The first colonial exploration projects took place in the central basin between 1952 and 1956, followed by prospecting by Esso–Texaco from 1974 to 1976. Japan National Oil Corporation conducted another exploration campaign in 1984. The main conclusion of these prospecting campaigns was that there is an absence of active petroleum systems.[13] More recently, a Brazilian petroleum company (High Resolution Technology) was hired to re-evaluate the same samples and data. Their more positive conclusions were, it seems, politically motivated, to attract potential investors.

Exploration took place along the Atlantic Ocean and Congo River estuary in the 1960s and in eastern Congo starting in the 1990s. An official Congolese research report published in 1970 made no mention of hydrocarbon potential in the east, which highlights both ignorance about the resource and its comparative newness in the region's inventory of natural wealth.[14]

Despite being underexploited and poorly regulated, oil is nevertheless a major contributor to the national treasury. It is the third most important export earner (at 11 per cent), after copper (51 per cent) and cobalt (30 per cent), and is well ahead of diamonds (3.4 per cent) and gold (1.2 per cent).[15] The Anglo-French company Perenco, which took over Chevron's activities in 1980, is the only company exploiting oil in Congo today. It pumps from hundreds of onshore and offshore wells.

Despite this national production, all of Congo's oil needs are covered by imports. In the immediate post-independence years, industrial development triggered increased demand for refined petroleum products. It was logical, then, that the country invest in the construction of a refinery. Discussions were launched in 1963 with Italian partners, resulting in the inauguration of the SOZIR refinery in 1968 in Muanda. SOZIR (Société Zairo-Italienne de Raffinage) was subsequently re-baptised SOCIR (Société Congo-Italienne de Raffinage, and then Société Congolaise des Industries de Raffinage). Like many other Zairian industrial white elephants, the refinery was handicapped by some inherent weaknesses. It has a nominal refining capacity of 750,000 cubic tonnes of crude per year but never operated at more than 50 per cent of this capacity. The crude that was refined in the past had to be imported (originally from Iran and then mainly from Nigeria) because domestic crude is too heavy for the SOCIR facility. Surprise nationalisation in the mid-1970s was a major setback. The refinery operated in fits and starts, with closures in 1988 and 1995, and ceased all refining activities in 1999. Co-owned by the state and the Swiss-based commodities giant Glencore (which is also active in Katanga's mining sector), SOCIR nevertheless fulfils the crucial economic activity of transporting imported oil by barge from offshore tankers to its onshore storage tanks.

A SOCIR sister parastatal, SEP-Congo (Services des Entreprises Pétrolières Congolaises), is responsible for all additional oil logistics. Its main task is the storage and supply of refined petroleum products throughout the country. It is therefore incumbent on SEP to keep the motors of the country's cars and lorries running. As households and companies replace their reliance on the Société Nationale d'Électricité (SNEL) for electricity with their use of generators, they increasingly depend on SEP for fuel supplies. But supply possibilities are not easy in terms of logistics, infrastructure, human resources and financing. Many large cities are undersupplied, placing a crushing burden on an already inadequate transportation system. SEP operates *à la congolaise*: inadequately, slowly and haphazardly. Private operators sometimes fill the gap when SEP is unable to keep supplies moving. In addition to its recourse to the country's road, rail and river transport network –which is badly in need of maintenance and modernisation – SEP has a 350-kilometre small-diameter oil pipeline running from Matadi to Kinshasa. The collection of customs duties and taxes from petroleum imports also falls under SEP's mandate.

The institutional and regulatory framework

As oil production is new to the DRC's economic landscape, its institutional and regulatory framework suffers from policy ambiguity and immaturity. It has often been said that Congo was not ready for independence in 1960. The fact that it took seven years for an independent Congo to pass its first law[16] regulating both mining and hydrocarbons (meaning oil and natural gas) is an example of this lack of preparedness. This first piece of legislation was nullified and replaced by a subsequent law in 1981[17] – at a time when Zaire's economy had temporarily rebounded after a devastating collapse of the copper economy in the mid to late 1970s. Through this updated legal framework, the government tried to affirm its will to develop the oil sector in partnership with international companies that had both the financial and technical capacities which the Zairian state did not possess.[18] Legislation, however, did not really help, because the political and economic context – dominated by mining – was still not conducive to the promotion of hydrocarbons.

Under the auspices of the World Bank, a new Mining Code was drafted and signed into law in 2002. It separated the regulation of mining and hydrocarbons.[19] Since then, the hydrocarbon sector has been in a state of regulatory limbo because it is governed by the 1981 legislation; this dates back to the Mobutu period, when oil was far from being a national priority. This old legislation was ill suited to the current context because of the emerging contribution that oil is making to the Congolese economy compared with 35 years ago, and also due to the changing role of African oil in the global economy.[20] A new Oil Code has been drafted and was approved recently, updating the 1981 legislation.[21] This new code, like the 1981 law, reflects the state's desire to exercise sovereignty over these important resources while also presenting some innovative elements. It seeks to have an overview of all scientific research about hydrocarbons and it recognises international health, environmental and security norms. The customs and fiscal contexts have also been revamped and the rights and responsibilities of decentralised administrations and local populations are recognised. In theory, the Oil Code tries to address the issue of transparency by establishing public tenders to award exploration and exploitation blocks. It also stipulates that a fund should be created for the financial benefit of future generations. However, these declarations of improved governance need to be viewed with some scepticism; lessons learned from Chad can be quite useful in this context.[22]

Final endorsement of the Oil Code has been a slow process. The Senate accepted it in 2013 and the National Assembly adopted it in June 2015. Some 127 articles were presented, analysed and discussed by parliamentarians who lack the necessary understanding of the financial, technical, geo-strategic, social and environmental dimensions of a complex set of propositions. Some articles are particularly sensitive, including the ones dealing with bonus payments (article 2), sovereignty over the continental shelf (article 3), or the possibility of carrying out oil activities in protected areas (article 26). Decentralisation politics also haunt the debate because the oil-generating province of Bas-Congo and other potential oil producers want to make sure that their interests will be protected. Important lobbying efforts by the World Wide Fund for Nature (WWF) and Global Witness contributed to delaying the Code's endorsement because they argued that the transparency clauses do not go far enough to curb corruption and protect the environment. Although now approved by parliament, the Code has not become law because it has not been signed by President Kabila.

Modifications in the legal framework have been taking place while the institutional context also evolves. The Ministry of Hydro-carbons was first set up as an independent ministry in May 2007. Hydrocarbons had previously been regulated by the Ministry of Energy (although an oil department was established in the Ministry of Energy in 1983) and, before that, by the Ministry of Mines. The Ministry works in tandem with Congolaise des Hydrocarbures (CoHydro), a state-owned company set up by Laurent-Désiré Kabila in 1999 to replace PetroCongo. CoHydro's declared aim was petroleum independence for the DRC, especially given the flurry of promising exploration prospects. CoHydro is the operational branch of the oil sector, responsible for exploration, production, import, export, transportation, storage, distribution and sales.

Regional oil politics

Oil is a particularly sensitive geo-political factor in Congo's relations with its neighbours. Congo's recent history with both Angola and Uganda is tainted with conflicts over oil exploitation.

According to François Misser, Angolo-Congolese oil relations constitute a 'sustainable disagreement' embedded in a tenuous power struggle dominated by Luanda.[23] Congo's principal known oil reserves are located along its narrow 37-kilometre outlet to the Atlantic Ocean, sandwiched between the Angolan mainland and its Cabinda exclave. Angola's productive oil blocks lie in disputed territorial waters whose boundaries were first drawn at the Berlin Conference in 1885. Chevron-Texaco has been pumping oil from these profitable blocks for Angola since 1968.

President Mobutu, who sided with rebel leader Jonas Savimbi during the Angolan civil war, was not overly preoccupied by Angolan oil activities, mainly because minerals were his regime's exclusive export priority – and main lifeline. Laurent-Désiré Kabila was heavily dependent upon Angolan military support during both the first war of liberation leading to the overthrow of Mobutu and subsequently during the second war against Rwanda and Uganda. He therefore chose not to make waves over oil. This partly explains Thomas Turner's assessment that 'DRC has paid a heavy price for its debt to the Angolan regime'.[24] The circumstances surrounding Laurent-Désiré Kabila's assassination remain unknown but there is speculation that Luanda was probably involved because Kabila had entered into diamond-trading agreements with Savimbi,[25] something that the Luanda authorities could not accept. Joseph Kabila, in turn, also decided to placate Luanda in exchange for military support during the second Congo war and then in the wake of the 2006 contested elections. Luanda buttressed Kabila's Republican Guard during deadly clashes with Jean-Pierre Bemba's militia in Kinshasa in March 2006.[26] As Joseph Kabila gradually consolidated his power base, relations between these two very large African countries remained tense.

In an attempt to appease diplomatic relations – and specifically to resolve the problems of compensation and rights over the contested offshore oilfields – presidents José Eduardo dos Santos and Joseph Kabila agreed to set up an economic common interest zone. Discussions started in 2003. Luanda ratified the agreement in 2004 and Kinshasa in November 2007. The delay in Kinshasa occurred for various reasons. The agreement was perceived as providing greater benefits to Angola in terms of revenues. As geographic limits were imprecise and explicit information about the extent of reserves was inadequate, some vocal members of the Congolese political establishment remained sceptical of the terms of the agreement. This was exacerbated by the fact that they were well aware that Angola has become an economic powerhouse, an African military superpower and Africa's second-largest oil producer, in part because of oil extraction from contested fields in blocks 14 and 15.[27] Angola produces around 1.8 million barrels per day from all of its oilfields and approximately 800,000 barrels per day from blocks 14 and 15. Officials in Kinshasa claim that around one-third of this production belongs to Congo.[28] While the claim is economically and diplomatically unrealistic, it makes political sense domestically because there are so many undeniable examples of the illegal exploitation of Congo's natural resources by its neighbours.[29] The setting up of this common interest zone has not clarified the border disagreement, however. While the agreement stipulates that new production revenues will be divided fifty–fifty, the question of retroactive compensation for decades of previous extraction remains unanswered. Production has never started in the zone, partly because of this disagreement.

Nessergy, a company owned by Dan Gertler's Fleurette Group, was instrumental in helping the Congolese government set up the common interest zone. This enabled Nessergy to acquire rights to rich offshore fields in 2006 for a relatively insignificant $500,000. The purchase, which was purely speculative, was arranged without public tender. Nessergy sold its rights back to the DRC in 2012. Global Witness, which has convincingly demonstrated the close business ties between Israeli billionaire Dan Gertler, President Joseph Kabila and the late Katumba Mwanke, reported that the purchase price was probably hundreds of times higher than the original $500,000 and claimed that there was a serious risk of corruption and non-transparency.[30]

As Congolese military dependency on Angola diminished, Kinshasa adopted an increasingly aggressive stance on oil rights. In May 2009, for example, Kinshasa lodged a complaint with the United Nations, accusing Angola of illegally violating Congo's continental shelf. If managed well, Congo could win the case because it is based on realistic projections of the maritime borders. There was a similar precedent when Cameroon won a case against Nigeria over disputed borders in the Bakassi area.

Over a thousand kilometres away from the Atlantic Ocean oilfields, a closely related incident followed in Kahemba. Military skirmishes took place over competing boundary claims in the diamond-rich border area south of Congo's Bandundu province and Angola's Lunda Norte province. This resulted, first, in massive expulsions of Congolese diamond diggers from Angola in 2009 and 2010 and then, in tit-for-tat retaliation, Kinshasa deported thousands of Angolans. While negotiations about sharing oil revenues now appear to be on hold, it is clear that the Angolans have maintained the upper hand in their oil relations with the DRC.

Oil relations between Kinshasa and Kampala have been even tenser than those with Luanda. Uganda and Congo were at war from August 1998 until July 2003 in a conflict that constituted one of the nastiest phases of violence in the DRC's recent history. This period overlapped with extensive oil prospecting in Uganda – including in disputed border areas with the DRC. As long as there were no major economic stakes to rattle political emotions, the border that had resulted from colonial arrangements did not seem to matter much. Today, however, given the discovery of significant reserves, the artificial line that runs through Lake Edward is under close scrutiny. Oil, according to Dominic Johnson, was one of the reasons why Uganda was a major military protagonist in the Ituri conflict. Deliberately maintaining insecurity in Ituri was a political objective of Ugandan President Museveni because it could help prevent 'the emergence of a strong Congolese voice which could effectively counter Ugandan claims to the oil area'.[31] The extent of the brutality in Ituri reinforces Paivi Lujala's analysis about conflicts tending to be more deadly when they overlap with oil.[32]

Uganda's oil activities have a direct impact on Congo's oil sector in the eastern part of the country.[33] Exploration was launched in Uganda by Heritage Oil in 1997. Heritage, which ultimately sold out to the UK-based Tullow Oil, describes itself as a company that 'typically focuses on regions which may have been overlooked and where it can participate as an early entrant'.[34] Heritage and Kinshasa discussed exploration on the Congo side of Lake Albert in 2002 but nothing happened at the time because of ongoing armed conflict. Heritage was founded by the 'financially astute'[35] former British mercenary Tony Buckingham, who had worked with Executive Outcomes, the notorious South African private security company. Executive Outcomes fought against Angolan rebel leader Jonas Savimbi on behalf of the Luanda government and in Sierra Leone to secure the government's access to its diamond fields, which were threatened by Revolutionary United Front guerrillas.[36] Buckingham's security expertise was an advantage for his negotiations and dealings with belligerents both on the ground and in ministerial offices.

Heritage got lucky in Uganda. They struck oil on the Ugandan side of the Lake Albert Rift Basin in 2006. The country's proven crude oil reserves are now estimated at 2.5 billion barrels according to the US Energy Information Administration.[37] Tullow's estimates are lower – 1.7 billion barrels. Tullow (which took over Heritage's activities in 2009), France's Total and the China National Offshore Oil Corporation (CNOOC) are the main actors in exploration and development today. The three companies are targeting gross oil production of at least 200,000 barrels per day in Uganda's Lake Albert Rift Basin.[38] This is eight times more than the DRC's current output. Uganda does not produce oil yet but production is expected to start in 2017 or 2018. Some will be refined domestically and some will be exported by pipeline to Lamu or Mombasa on Kenya's Indian Ocean coast.

Oil was a prominent discussion topic in Ngurdoto, Tanzania during a 2007 meeting between presidents Museveni and Kabila. Jakaya Kikwete, the president of Tanzania, brokered what was then expected to be an important post-conflict engagement between the former belligerents. An agreement was signed, including clauses directly and indirectly related to oil. A commission was set up to resolve border disputes – most importantly on the contested Rukwanzi Island in Lake Albert, where troops from both countries were stationed, and in the Mahagi area. 'Both countries also agreed that oil fields straddling the border would be jointly explored and exploited.'[39] The Ngurdoto agreement and its Dar es Salaam follow-up meeting in 2008 are concrete illustrations of failed diplomacy. Not only have the agreements remained dead letters but the situation has become more complicated and embittered as a result of a series of aborted prospecting deals.

Rights to blocks 1 and 2 on the Congo side of Lake Albert have been awarded, rescinded and re-awarded since 2002. Four different Congolese oil ministers have granted them to four different consortia.[40] This underscores the political nature of the negotiations and the high economic expectations. The first award to Heritage in 2002 gave the company exploration rights in a swathe of territory about the size of Belgium. In 2006 a new deal was signed with Heritage and Tullow. Another short-lived award was subsequently signed in 2008 with South Africa's Divine Inspiration Group. Bonuses are generally paid for prospecting rights in the oil business. Signature bonuses could have amounted to $3 million, which partially explains the multiple awards by new ministers.[41] There is also a geo-strategic explanation. Not allowing Tullow to explore on the Congolese side of the lake was a deliberate strategic move to undermine Ugandan capacity to move forward with prospecting and ultimately drilling. This contributed to maintaining tensions between Kinshasa and Kampala as it vitiated the plan to explore jointly for oil as stipulated in the Ngurdoto agreement. The fatal shooting of a Heritage engineer from Britain in August 2007 by Congolese soldiers was a low point in oil relations between the two countries.[42] Carl Nefdt was carrying out research for Heritage in a disputed border zone on the lake when he was killed. Kinshasa was not keen to see Uganda develop into a powerful petro state because new wealth for Uganda was perceived as potentially contributing to a power imbalance in the region. A precedent had already been established in Angola, to the detriment of the DRC.

In 2010, Joseph Kabila finally signed a presidential decree awarding the exploration contract to two little-known companies: Caprikat and Foxwhelp. This award sparked cries of corruption and foul play, tarnishing investor confidence in Congo even further. No one really knows who controls Caprikat and Foxwhelp. Mossack Fonseca and Company, a Panamanian law firm, registered them in the British Virgin Islands, a haven of corporate anonymity. Although the exact ownership is ambiguous, the *Financial Times* quoted the Oil Minister as saying that Dan Gertler was associated with the two companies.[43] It was generally believed that Gertler and Katumba Mwanke were behind this award. Antoine Ghonda, a close Kabila ally, is also said to have been involved.[44] The South African press reported that Khulubuse Zuma, President Jacob Zuma's nephew, and the president's legal adviser Michael Hulley owned Caprikat and Foxwhelp.[45] The deployment of South African troops in the Intervention Brigade set up by the United Nations in March 2013 to reinforce MONUSCO (the United Nations peacekeeping and stabilisation operation in Congo) in eastern DRC is an indication of President Zuma's motivation to stabilise the region for economic reasons.[46] South Africa is also present in Congo's oil sector through its firm Engen Petroleum Ltd, which is a major petroleum distributor.

In August 2014, Oil of DRCongo, a company owned by Gertler acting on behalf of Caprikat and Foxwhelp, announced a discovery on the Congo side of Lake Albert of more than 3 billion barrels.[47]

This is an amount comparable to the proven oil reserves of Britain and South Sudan and could translate into a production capacity of 50,000 barrels per day – double what the country already produces. Oil of DRCongo has invested more than $75 million in seismic exploration and plans to prepare for the drilling of two exploration wells by building infrastructure and relocating local communities. The company claims that this discovery would expand Congo's economy by 25 per cent. It is difficult to say if this is myth or reality. It seems, however, that this announcement is most likely a public relations ploy orchestrated by Oil of DRCongo to spark interest in the area so that the company can sell off its stakes.

The pattern that is evolving in eastern Congo is typical of the oil sector elsewhere in Africa. Small companies take prospecting initiatives and, if they are successful, sell out to larger, more experienced firms. But the flurry of activity around prospecting and concession awards does not translate easily into production and revenues. Before eastern Congo can start producing oil, the pipeline question needs to be resolved. There are two options: 1) the DRC and Uganda negotiate the possibility of transporting Congo's oil via Uganda's pipeline; and 2) the Congolese lay their own pipeline across the entire central basin for export through Atlantic coast terminals. While the first option makes the most sense in terms of costs and benefits, the Congolese government is reluctant to enter into a relationship of dependency with their inimical neighbour. They have vaguely expressed a preference for the more expensive and less pragmatic option for reasons of national sovereignty. Given the distance and geographical constraints, this pipeline will certainly never be built. The Italian company Italcon RDC signed a memorandum of understanding with the government in 2011 to study the feasibility of creating an oil pipeline network. 'Reptilian', the project's name, never got off the drawing board.[48] One sceptic has been rather blunt about this: 'If the Congolese can't build a road across the country, how the hell will they be able to build and secure a transnational pipeline?'[49] In addition, the Congolese will need to be attentive to the types of security problems common along the Nigerian pipeline network, such as vandalism, sabotage and theft.[50]

In reality, there has been relatively little debate about this issue, given its rather long-term time frame. Congo's political economy is driven by immediate or short-term perspectives, not by the kind of long-term vision that is needed here. A comparison with the Chad–Cameroon pipeline could be useful in this context, especially with regard to the multiple caveats that need to be taken into account. Douglas Yates' assessment that the Chad–Cameroon pipeline 'symbolized the many problems of the African oil sector: foreign domination, export orientation, environmental pollution and grievances of indigenous peoples, rent-seeking, political corruption, and violent conflict' could be a prediction of things to come in DRC's oil sector.[51]

The Virunga oil saga

A particularly seedy episode in the story of Congo's environmental paradox is the ongoing oil saga in the Virunga National Park. To drill or not to drill, that is the focus of an angry debate. Eighty-five per cent of the park is now under concession for oil production. Established in 1925, Virunga is Africa's oldest park. It has an amazing variety of landscapes, including forests, savannahs, rivers, lakes, marshlands, volcanoes and even glaciers. It is home to approximately 200 critically endangered mountain gorillas, in addition to a rich mix of other mammals, reptiles, birds and plants. The Virunga fiasco, however, is not unique. Oil blocks have also been mapped out in Africa's largest protected area, the Salonga National Park.

Virunga's estimated annual economic value is $48.9 million without oil, and if the security situation improves it could be more than $1.1 billion.[52] This figure, it must be added, is biased because it is in WWF's interest to boost the value of the park for public relations purposes. Calculations are based on direct-use value (mainly tourism and fishing), indirect value (mainly carbon sequestration) and mostly non-use value (described vaguely as 'future use').

In addition to carrying out sustained lobbying efforts, Congo's international partners (mainly the European Commission) have invested large amounts of money in the conservation of this important biodiversity hotspot over the past 20 years. Virunga has been a refugee sanctuary in the wake of the Rwandan genocide, the theatre of violent bloodletting, and subject to severe management problems during this period.[53] The latest calamity there is the discovery of oil. Advocates in favour of oil activities argue – unpersuasively – that extraction, environmental protection and social well-being can be compatible. However, there are inadequate institutional and governance safeguards to back up these claims. Threats of wildlife loss, pollution, social turmoil and corruption seem more likely.

In 2006, SOCO International signed a joint venture contract with the Congolese government and Dominion Petroleum to explore for oil in and around the Virunga Park. The government subsequently granted additional oil concessions to France's Total and South Africa's SacOil (South Africa Congo Oil), although SOCO is the only company currently active within the confines of the park. Despite international non-governmental organisation (NGO) and local Congolese activism, Joseph Kabila signed a presidential decree in June 2010 allowing SOCO, Dominion and CoHydro to pursue their oil activities in Virunga. In Congolese law, a presidential decree carries more weight than a concession agreement. The decree was the green light SOCO lobbied for, but, conversely, the panic signal conservationists dreaded. SOCO's environmental impact assessment made no reference to the park's status as a protected area, which is not a good omen.

Former Environment Minister José Endundo vacillated over the issue. He emphasised that national sovereignty was sacrosanct: the Congolese alone are to determine how national resources should be used to guarantee benefits to the Congolese people. But he also appeared sensitive to the international uproar. This led him to temporarily ban SOCO's activities in December 2010. In yet another reverse decision in October 2011, SOCO received a permit to explore for oil in block 5, much of which is near the endangered gorilla habitat.

NGO concerns have been echoed by top-ranking diplomatic figures such as UNESCO's General Secretary, the World Bank's country representative and the European Union's ambassador to Kinshasa.[54] Spearheaded by Belgian MP George Dallemagne, his fellow lawmakers have also been involved in the debate. The Belgian Federal Parliament adopted a resolution in November 2012 urging the Congolese, French and British governments to oppose any actions that could be detrimental to the park.[55] One of the world's richest families, the Buffetts, has proactively supported development projects in and around the park.[56]

Parliamentarians from Kivu are strongly in favour of oil production in the park because of perceived development benefits. They contend – unconvincingly – that other countries have granted concessions in national parks and have been able to reconcile environmental protection with people's rights to benefit from natural resources.[57] In a blatant case of conflict of interest, Célestin Vunabandi, a member of parliament representing North Kivu, was on the SOCO payroll as a consultant.[58] Kivu civil society organisations, however, are firmly opposed to the plan. Pollution risks are a legitimate fear: oil extraction in Bas-Congo has already taken its toll on the environment because of 'poor maintenance of pipelines, gas flaring and dumping of waste'.[59]

The ambiguous legal framework is a constraint on reaching an agreement. According to some interpretations, Congolese law bans mining and oil exploitation in national parks.[60] But SOCO found an apparent loophole, which affirms that scientific activities are allowed in protected areas. The Congolese authorities concede that they signed agreements with UNESCO putting Virunga on the World Heritage Site list in 1969 and on the World Heritage

Site in Danger list in 1994. Nevertheless, they are also toying with the United Nations' General Assembly resolution 1514 (XV) of 14 December 1960, which states that 'peoples may, for their own ends, freely dispose of their natural wealth and resources without prejudice to any obligations arising out of international economic co-operation, based upon the principle of mutual benefit, and international law'.[61] This legal ambiguity could conveniently be avoided by redrawing the boundaries of the park. This is something that UNESCO says is possible. The Australians have expressed interest in doing the same thing in their Tasmanian Wilderness World Heritage Area. Similarly, UNESCO has approved boundary changes in the Selous Game Reserve in Tanzania to accommodate uranium mining.[62]

The spring of 2014 was full of drama in the Virunga Park. SOCO carried out seismic surveys and exploratory drilling as the security services, in support of SOCO, beefed up their presence and surveillance in the area to silence opposition voices. NGO activists reported increased harassment of local populations, particularly fishing communities in the vicinity of Lake Edward. Even Catholic missionaries, who are usually immune to such problems, complained of administrative hassles. The same month, armed men shot and seriously wounded the park's head warden, the charismatic (but controversial)[63] Belgian Prince Emmanuel de Merode, who has been an active and outspoken critic of oil activities in the park. The shooting took place on the day he met with officials in the Goma public prosecutor's office to deposit a legal complaint against SOCO. One of the items in the complaint related to the bullying of local populations by SOCO subcontractors, a situation well documented in the prize-winning documentary film *Virunga*.[64] (This is another instance of celebrity interest in the DRC. Hollywood star Leonardo DiCaprio is the film's executive producer and former president Bill Clinton went to see it at a high-society showing in New York.)[65] A similar complaint is about to be lodged in London with the Serious Fraud Office. The Belgian ambassador to Kinshasa described the attack as a 'seemingly targeted ambush' in a confidential cable, and Belgian parliamentarian Chevalier François-Xavier de Donnea said that the coincidence was 'extremely worrisome'.[66]

The UNESCO World Heritage Committee met in Doha, Qatar in June 2014. Another 'conflict of interest' case almost transpired when the Congolese official delegation to the meeting asked SOCO to pay for their trip. SOCO claims to have turned down the request.[67] SOCO pledged to end its oil prospecting activities in Virunga just prior to the meeting – until UNESCO and the Congolese government agreed that their activities were not incompatible with World Heritage conditions. This, however, is not exactly a happy denouement. SOCO needs time to interpret the data from the surveys and will most likely find some kind of accommodation with the government to pursue oil activities if the results are positive. There are various possible ways in which drilling could proceed in block 5 despite the SOCO–WWF agreement. SOCO could, for example, sell the block to another company. Although the economic stakes are too high to imagine a withdrawal, 'there is still a long way to go before understanding the real potential of the zone, since the drilling phase might not take place for years'.[68]

Conclusion

There is a strong likelihood that Congo will try to further develop its oil production. Despite a broad range of challenges – an inhibiting regional political context, inadequate transportation infrastructure and limited technical knowledge, among others – opportunities exist too. There are known reserves, appropriate extraction technology, global demand, geo-political imperatives to diversify supply sources and nascent investor interest. Africa's participation in the global oil market has already firmly taken root, and this offers favourable economy-of-scale possibilities. The real question is not *if* the sector will develop, but *when*. The subsidiary question is how the oil business will be managed. The assessment that 'it is not because

Congo is a corrupt country that it is absurd to imagine an oil boom' seems appropriate and pragmatic.[69]

Unlike the three previous chapters about the renewable resources of forests, agricultural land and water, where there are unequivocal interconnections, this chapter has focused on a non-renewable enclave sector with fewer obvious environmental links. Some recurring political economy patterns do exist, however, especially with respect to mining. Secrecy, for example, characterises both the oil and the mining sectors. There are many things that remain obscure, such as information about profits, who really owns companies, who are the deal makers and how concession awards are negotiated. Both sectors are run directly from the top, meaning by the president and his close allies. This is a paradox because Congolese law gives the president the power to make important decisions about oil and mineral exploitation, but, in doing so, it also institutionalises non-transparent management arrangements – a situation analysed in the following chapter on mining.

Congo's political economy is clearly not conducive to Norwegian-style oil management with sustainable fiscal policies, stakeholder involvement, environmental protection, links with other sectors in the economy and a judicious balance between savings and spending – quite the contrary, in fact. Ian Taylor's assessment of Africa's oil sector in general could well be a foreboding message about the specifically Congolese context: 'Africa's past is replete with examples where windfall gains from oil have not been utilised for the common good and in the service of broad-based sustainable development. Furthermore, the reproduction of the continent's dependency on primary commodities is hardly something to be celebrated.'[70]

Congo's oil sector is embedded in a brutal tradition of natural resource extraction and exploitation. Given the absence of democratic governance and economic development, Congolese oil will continue to figure as a coveted prize for top decision makers – once again to the detriment of social progress and the environment.

Chapter 6

MINING: RISE, DECLINE AND RENAISSANCE

Introduction

Mining in Congo is a multifaceted activity with ramifications for the macroeconomic situation of the country, social issues, security concerns, regional politics and the environment. Minerals play a fundamental role in the Congolese political economy and determine Congo's place in international relations. Over a century ago, the Belgian geologist Jules Cornet justifiably described Katanga as a 'geological scandal'. Experts still voice that assessment. New age prospectors dream of striking it rich there, tempted by imagined opportunities. Rumours that Congo's minerals could be worth up to $24 trillion circulate via the internet, and even in usually serious journals such as *Foreign Policy*.[1] But this is just as much a myth as it is fantasy economics. There is simply insufficient geological information to make such a wild assertion, according to hard-headed geologists. The mining sector has been expanding rapidly over the past decade. It is extremely dynamic due to global demand, new technologies, innovative prospecting techniques, increased regional security, pressure for a more appropriate regulatory framework and the involvement of crowds of actors that come and go. Because of this dynamism, the sector is very different today than it was 20 years ago and will certainly evolve significantly over the next 20 years.

These are some of the issues addressed in this chapter, which also illustrates how artisanal and industrial mining have been experiencing tremendous changes resulting from new governance networks, local and regional politicking, and the global demand for base, precious and strategic minerals. After an introductory section that provides data about Congo's known reserves, an historical summary follows, spanning the years of colonial mining paternalism and the Mobutu period of decline, which continued under Laurent-Désiré Kabila. The next sections present the debates about artisanal mining and conflict minerals. These lead into a discussion of the strengths and weaknesses of the new regulatory framework. The chapter draws to a close by arguing that the sector has entered a fragile renaissance phase and concludes with an overview of future prospects. This last chapter on mining also helps put the previous ones into perspective with regard to the links and interdependencies between the sectors themselves and within the overarching governance context.

Congo is the world's largest producer of cobalt ore and is a major producer of copper and industrial diamonds. It also has gold, silver, tantalum, tin, zinc and uranium. These are but a few of its 1,100 mineral substances.[2] Table 6.1 shows the considerable strategic significance of some of them.[3] Minerals play a role in the political economy of every Congolese province, as illustrated in Table 6.2. Political and media discussion about Congo's minerals often neglects the importance of quarry products, which are geologically related. In a country that resembles a vast worksite with construction and public works projects on the increase (driven by population growth and pockets of development), cement, sand, stone and clay for brick making are also of significant economic importance. This explains the building of the new Nyumba Ya Akiba cement-manufacturing facility in Bas-Congo, a joint venture between Lucky Cement of Pakistan and the Congolese Rawji Group, funded by the African Development Bank.[4] They are betting on the future construction of Inga III, which would create a huge demand for cement in the area.

Congo's ores are very much part of today's high-tech economy and are inextricably linked to the 'global greed for gadgets'.[6] Minerals scraped from the earth by someone's bare hands end up

Table 6.1 Currently known world reserves and rank of Congo's minerals

Mineral	Percentage of known world reserves	World rank
Cobalt	46.05	1
Industrial diamonds	11.23	1
Iron	5.83	2
Copper	10.77	4
Coltan	6.74	5
Gold	2.70	7
Cassiterite	2.85	8
Magnesium	0.17	9

Source: Mupepele Monti (2012: 294).

Table 6.2 Mineral deposits by province

Province	Minerals
Bandundu	Diamonds, gold, petroleum
Bas-Congo	Bauxite, shale oil, limestone, phosphates, vanadium, diamonds, gold
Equateur	Iron, copper, gold, diamonds
Kasaï-Oriental	Diamonds, iron, silver, nickel, tin
Kasaï-Occidental	Diamonds, gold, magnesium, chrome, nickel
Katanga	Copper, cobalt, magnesium, limestone, uranium, tin, coal
Maniema	Tin, diamonds, tin, coltan
North Kivu	Gold, niobium, tantalum, tin, beryl, tungsten, monazite
Orientale	Gold, diamonds, iron
South Kivu	Gold, niobium, tantalum, tin, sapphire

Sources: World Bank (2008: 14); Royal Museum for Central Africa archives.

in the most sophisticated technology imaginable. Coltan,[7] a metal found in mobile phones, laptop computers and tablets, is mined in the eastern provinces and is considered by the US government to be a conflict mineral.[8] While Congo does indeed have some strategic minerals, these substances can also be found elsewhere. Congo's coltan reserves appear to be far smaller than often indicated. Some media sources and non-governmental organisations (NGOs) refer to the far-fetched figure of 70 per cent of world reserves, but credible geological sources place it much lower.[9] This exaggeration was based on old information that did not include discoveries of coltan reserves in China, Chile and Australia. It is also part of a recurring pattern whereby geological reality is manipulated for public consumption to draw attention to political and humanitarian problems, notably in eastern Congo. Private companies also play with figures to stimulate investor interest.

These minerals also play an obvious role in industry. A medium-sized car contains around 1.5 kilometres of copper wire, for example. Only Chile has more copper than Katanga. Congo has nearly half of the world's cobalt, a mineral vital for the manufacture of jet engines. Cobalt is listed as a 'particularly strategic' mineral for the US defence sector.[10] During World War II, uranium for the Manhattan Project, used to make the atomic bombs that devastated Hiroshima and Nagasaki, came from the Shinkolobwe mine in the mineral-rich Katanga province.

Western governments are concerned about consistent access to minerals. However, for minerals from Congo, this is probably a relatively minor risk. Throughout the country's troubled past, supply has never been disrupted significantly. A far greater danger is Congo's minerals, particularly uranium, getting into the wrong hands, notably those of Iran or the Lebanese Hezbollah. The United States and regulatory agencies such as the International Atomic Energy Agency appear unable to control the illegal trade networks involved in extracting uranium from cobalt ore. Chinese, North Korean, Pakistani, Indian and Lebanese traders are suspected of involvement in the trade of uranium ore exploited by artisanal diggers in Katanga. Urine samples of these miners reveal abnormally high concentrations of uranium[11] – which proves that they are in contact with the substance. It is not improbable that Lebanese Hezbollah groups are involved in uranium exports to Iran, which helps explain why the United States Department of the Treasury has sanctioned a

Lebanese businessman active in Congo who is allegedly a Hezbollah financier.[12] The Italian mafia is also known to have been involved in uranium smuggling from Congo.[13]

Congo's mining sector is full of paradoxes, lost opportunities and inconsistencies. Potential vast underground reserves are underexploited because of insufficient investment in infrastructure and because geological information is inadequate. More geological information is held in Belgium's Royal Museum for Central Africa, and to a lesser extent at the French Geological Survey (Bureau de Recherches Géologiques et Minières), than in Congo itself. Mining is heavily dependent on transportation networks and electricity – both of which are woefully inadequate. Robust growth in the sector over the past few years has not translated into poverty reduction. Ordinary people express this by saying: 'Our beds should be of gold and diamonds, but we are just sleeping on straw mats.' Another tragic inconsistency is the fact that mineral wealth benefits a small cluster of political and military elites and foreign companies but hardly contributes to national development. Despite major efforts to make the mining business more transparent, the roles of President Kabila's family, his close allies (such as Dan Gertler) and Chinese partners remain shrouded in mystery. In terms of macro-level policy design, the expected role of the state in the reform process has been somewhat puzzling because it is perceived as being part of the problem and part of the solution at the same time.

Historical overview

Mining is an ancient activity in Congo. Copper smelting, for example, dates back to the fifth century in what is today's Katanga.[14] In the late 1800s, European interest in Katanga – and that of King Leopold II – was apparently motivated by rumours of discovering gold, not copper.[15] Large-scale mineral prospecting and extraction started in the early twentieth century. It was based on a hegemonic concession system whereby private capital and the colonial state joined forces, cooperating, according to some, with the aim of 'plundering' Congo's minerals.[16] Copper became the new rubber for the Belgian colonial establishment and continued to be Congo's single most important industrial commodity for decades. Production started at the Etoile mine near Lubumbashi in 1909, spurted during World War I and became increasingly industrialised in the 1940s. Production peaked in the mid-1980s, hovering at around 500,000 tonnes per annum.[17]

The Union Minière du Haut-Katanga (UMHK) controlled the lucrative copper sector in Katanga and Symétain ran the tin mines in Maniema. The Société Minière du Bécéka had the diamonds fields of Kasaï and the Mines de Kilo-Moto produced gold in Ituri. These colossal, politically well-connected concession companies contributed greatly to the development of Belgium and to the fortunes of some of its citizens – including members of the royal family. American captains of industry, John D. Rockefeller for example, also profited from investments in these concession companies. State and company shared responsibility for the development and maintenance of infrastructure, particularly transportation and energy in and around their concessions. Concessions were operated like states within states and adhered to an industrial paternalistic philosophy.[18] The Catholic Church played an important role in this arrangement, not only through the official 'civilising mission'[19] but also by pacifying workers. Concessions were gilded utopias where, in addition to salaries, the company provided workers and their families with food, housing, schooling, spiritual guidance and entertainment. The well-being of workers and their families was judiciously calibrated to expectations of productivity and profit.

This huge social engineering endeavour had its advantages. In the immediate post-independence period, mining provided half of the state's revenues and between 70 per cent and 80 per cent of export earnings.[20] These results were based on the work of 87,000 labourers in around 40 concessions in the provinces of Kasaï, Katanga, Kivu, Maniema and Oriental.[21] The Union Minière alone had 20,000 workers (including 2,000 expatriates) and provided livelihoods to most of Katanga's population.[22] It was so vital to them, they referred to it as their father and mother.[23] When it collapsed in the late 1980s, they lamented that they had been turned into orphans.

Katanga's attempt to secede from the newly independent country was primarily related to minerals and machinations from elements within the Belgian colonial establishment to maintain control over them.[24] This coincided with the political ambitions of local elites to redistribute power and resources.[25] Independent Katanga chose the region's famous copper cross (*croisette*) as its national emblem. Along similar lines, shortly afterwards, in August 1960, secessionist leader Albert Kalonji declared the independence of the autonomous Mining State of South Kasaï, whose very name testifies to the interconnection between diamonds and politics.

In the aftermath of this first 'Congo crisis', President Mobutu nationalised the concession companies in an effort to consolidate his power base. The takeover in 1967 of the Union Minière (which was first renamed as Générale Congolaise des Mines – Gécomines – then Générale des Carrières et des Mines – Gécamines) and the other concession companies was an important landmark. The Société Générale de Belgique, the Banque de Bruxelles and the Empain group, which all held vast mining interests, gradually withdrew from the sector – and eventually from the country. These nationalisations opened up a new era of patrimonial politics by enabling Mobutu to appropriate mineral revenues. He used them to accumulate a personal fortune, invest in large industrial prestige projects (such as the Maluku steel plant, the Inga Dam and Inga–Shaba high-tension transmission line) and buy himself legitimacy as an African 'big man'. During this process, driven by the *autenticité* crusade he started for political reasons, Mobutu changed the country's name from Congo to Zaire and Katanga to Shaba – which means copper in Swahili.

The euphoria of independence and quest for economic sovereignty did not last long. By the mid-1970s, just after the wave of nationalisations, world copper prices plummeted, inflation soared and the Zaire currency lost value. Copper exports declined, equipment broke down and was not replaced. Investment in production dwindled as qualified staff were substituted by political appointees. All of these factors, exacerbated by mismanagement and corruption, led to the gradual disintegration of Gécamines. By 1990, when the once-productive Kamoto mine in Kolwezi literally caved in, many investors and policy experts surmised that Congo's large-scale copper industry was moribund and would never recover. This subsequently proved to be an expensive miscalculation.

State failure and the decline of industrial mining were connected. Both were entwined in a downward spiral. Ambitious World Bank structural adjustment programmes were not able to help. An International Monetary Fund team sent to Zaire in the late 1970s, led by Erwin Blumenthal, identified with astonishment how President Mobutu had cleverly robbed the country's mineral wealth for personal interests.[26] The pattern is still being reproduced today. Regimes may change but the strategies deployed by elites to control public resources for their personal benefit are firmly entrenched.[27] These strategies constitute an enduring obstacle to development and meaningful political change.

To compensate for diminishing industrial mining cash flows, Mobutu liberalised the gold and diamond sectors in 1982. By the end of his dictatorship, revenues earned from artisanal mining – mainly diamonds – had replaced those from copper and cobalt, whose extraction, processing, transportation and commercialisation require a functioning state apparatus and industrial support system. The Kasaï diamond fields thus replaced Katanga's ores as the regime's lifeline. Artisanal mining was more conducive to the kind of patrimonial control President Mobutu needed, especially as his erstwhile Western backers withdrew their support in the late 1980s when the Cold War drew to a close. Nevertheless, control of the artisanal diamond sector with its multiple actors remained elusive, largely because it represented 'a significant independent economic power'.[28]

As Laurent-Désiré Kabila marched to power in 1997, he also tried to take control of artisanal mining, particularly in eastern Congo. His mismanagement of the diamond fields of Kasaï devastated an already crippled Société Minière de Bakwanga (MIBA).[29] Military networks rapidly replaced the state as intermediaries between local producers and global users,[30] regulating access to artisanal mining sites, the workforce, production and trade.[31] This was one dimension of the process described by Vlassenroot and Raeymaekers as 'the transformation of regulation'.[32] Laurent-Désiré Kabila built up a war chest by awarding dubious mining contracts to his erstwhile foreign financers and to foreign investors – some more or less respectable, others clearly rogue. His deal-making strategy was based on secrecy, which enabled him to grant the same concession to various partners at the same time.[33] The objective was to earn multiple signature bonuses. Zimbabwean investors were well represented in the new deals. Billy Rautenbach, for example, a white Zimbabwean businessman with close ties to President Mugabe, was appointed head of Gécamines in November 1998, ostensibly as recompense for President Mugabe's military support.

The mining sector, which had been completely dominated by the monolithic colonial state system, became highly globalised under the Laurent-Désiré Kabila regime in a very short period of time, as new partners from multiple countries hoped for a bonanza. In a major shift, the main protagonists were no longer large multinationals but small exploration companies and mining 'juniors' without exploitation ambitions. The arrival of the juniors was first facilitated in 1995, when Mobutu's Prime Minister Kengo Wa Dondo paved the way for new joint venture strategies. The juniors' objectives included discovering new deposits, deal making and quick profit taking. This approach contrasts sharply with the business plans of mining majors (usually well-established Western companies), which tend to have a 30-year perspective. Hundreds of exploration permits were granted by Kabila in the late 1990s. This speculative tactic entailed gaining access to new concessions and eventually selling them off to the majors when the time was right, or securing financial backing to exploit them themselves. Few majors were active during the war years, unlike the juniors. Exploration and financial feasibility studies were badly needed because it was crucial to develop and update geological knowledge. Kabila realised this, and the juniors were happy to accommodate him. Originally and primarily involved in construction and public works, Groupe Forrest International is one of the few quasi-Belgian mining companies operating in the DRC today – having entered the mining sector in the 1990s.[34] The company is an important player in the DRC but a minor global actor.

Canadian juniors were particularly active during this phase; this can be explained by Canadian expertise worldwide in the mining sector and by favourable venture capital opportunities on the country's stock exchanges.[35] Export Development Canada (the country's export credit agency) also facilitated investment in international mining endeavours.[36] One high-profile Canadian deal turned into a real saga. In 2010, the DRC government nationalised First Quantum Minerals' Frontier copper mine, accusing the company of contract violation after it had already invested approximately $700 million in the concession. This is not the kind of message Congo should be sending to international investors, who remain very sensitive when it comes to uncertainties surrounding nationalisation. When First Quantum brought the case to international arbitration, it won. Two years later, Eurasian Natural Resources Corporation (founded in Kazakhstan but now registered in Luxembourg) bought the Canadian company's projects for $1.25 billion.[37]

Artisanal mining

As the formal industrial mining sector has declined over the past quarter of a century, artisanal and small-scale mining has started to flourish. Artisanal and small-scale mining is the Congo's most important mining activity today in terms of employment, though not state revenues. The way in which artisanal diggers have totally replaced industrial extraction in some areas testifies to the resilience of markets and producers as well as to political exigencies. It has, however, been a shift with a heavy social toll. Figures are unreliable but a significant percentage of mining production is carried out by artisanal diggers (*creuseurs*) working mostly with picks, shovels and sieves.[38] This is certainly the case for the '3Ts' (tin, tantalum, and tungsten) in the Kivus, but less so for copper and cobalt in Katanga. How many *creuseurs* are there? There is no way of knowing for sure, but rough estimates range from between half a million to 2 million men, women and children.[39] The Congolese Minister of Mines alluded to 1.2 million.[40] Even at half a million, this means that artisanal mining could be the second-largest employment sector after agriculture and there could be around as many workers as there are civil servants. Although the sector poses significant social and environmental problems, it is vital to the survival of millions of Congolese people – perhaps as many as 10 million.[41] As in other employment sectors in the DRC, one person's earnings are usually shared with multiple family members. Gold is mined by *creuseurs* in the Ituri district of Orientale province and the Kivus; coltan and cassiterite in the Kivus; diamonds in the two Kasaïs; and heterogenite (a cobalt ore) in Katanga.

Although each production situation has its particularities (artisanal mining is very different in the Kivus than in Katanga), there are recurring patterns common to many. Numerous children, for instance, work as *creuseurs*. Instead of going to school, they help their families dig, sort, wash and carry.[42] Nevertheless, the portrayal of children as victims in artisanal mining tends to be one-sided. From the opposite perspective, anthropologists such as André and Godin have showed how children use their earnings to become independent, constructing positive roles for themselves within their family structures and communities.[43] Likewise, Geenen observed that children working in mines in South Kivu used their earnings to pay for school fees,[44] something that their parents may be unable or unwilling to do. Women are also active in the artisanal sector, carrying out specific tasks such as washing, sorting and transporting ore.

Violence against women, prostitution and sexually transmitted diseases form an ongoing cluster of problems. Access to healthcare, sanitation and clean drinking water is limited and random. Food prices are inflated as farmers abandon their fields to dig for ores.[45] This type of mining, which can be carried out with little capital investment, is gruelling and can be very dangerous, especially given the absence of even basic safety equipment. Risks of cave-ins and suffocation are exacerbated by a disregard for fundamental rights and a lack of government oversight or NGO support. Long hours, seven days a week, are the norm. Although probably somewhat exaggerated, one NGO report qualified the living conditions of *creuseurs* as 'modern slavery', in part because they become indebted to the recruiting agents (*sponsors*) who facilitate their entry into the sector.[46] Rebel militias as well as government troops are actively involved in artisanal mining areas, profiting from the illegal taxation of *creuseurs*.[47]

Dependent on circumstances beyond their control, *creuseurs* are the weakest links in the networks that exploit them.[48] Their earnings are low, especially compared with those of the middlemen who buy locally and sell regionally or internationally.[49] It is uncommon for them to form efficient cooperatives or associations, although small teams of men and boys working together can be close-knit.[50] The areas where they operate tend to be highly militarised and predatory authorities are the only real manifestation of the state. Militias and factions from within the Congolese armed forces have been able to impose 'parallel systems of regulation and exploitation'[51] that put *creuseurs* in a particularly vulnerable situation. They have to pay high fees for protection and the right to work, including to people who may hold (or claim to hold) title to the concession where they work.

Sara Geenen's research among gold diggers in South Kivu showed that 'miners pay amounts up to several hundreds of dollars a week to different authorities (FARDC soldiers, Mining Police, intelligence officers, people in the mining administration and magistrates)'.[52] In some cases, the value of the bribes outweighs miners' profits.[53] Traditional chiefs can also demand a share of profits. Vulnerability was also documented among the Congolese diamond diggers working in Angola's Lunda Norte province. When crossing the border to go back to Congo, they were robbed by Angolan government troops who told them: 'You came empty handed, you leave empty handed.'[54] Although these examples indicate that *creuseurs* appear to be victims of extortion, it could also be argued that in many instances they find ways to outwit their predators and other actors in the mining business.[55]

The precarious environment of artisanal mining contrasts sharply with the benevolent paternalism of the late colonial industrial mining era and in some of today's industrial sites – because companies tend to be sensitive about their reputations in the framework of corporate social responsibility. In the context of artisanal mining, it is not surprising that the government is powerless to exercise real oversight or provide meaningful assistance. SAESSCAM (Service d'Assistance et d'Encadrement du Small Scale Mining), the government agency set up to assist artisanal and small-scale miners, is largely unable to implement its mandate. All of these problems, however, need to be viewed through the eyes of the *creuseurs* themselves, whose livelihood options are extremely limited. Despite the danger and vulnerability inherent to life in the mines, such a life also constitutes 'one of the few sources of ... hope for rural eastern Congolese'.[56]

Conflict minerals

Minerals – and their illegal exploitation – have definitely contributed to conflict in eastern DRC, exacerbating the more serious problem of access to land in densely populated areas. The socio-economic consequences have been dramatic. 'Mining and the conflict surrounding it have helped produce a social world that is extremely confusing and in which it is impossible to know what is going to happen from one day to the next.'[57] There is no doubt that Rwanda and Uganda, with the complicity of certain Congolese groups (including the military), have been actively involved.[58] But the links and subtle regional, ethnic, economic and political dynamics between conflict and minerals are far more complex than they are frequently portrayed. The commonly articulated message suggests that armed groups persist and terrorise local populations thanks to the sale of artisan-dug metals (mainly tantalum, tin, tungsten and gold) and that Western consumers can help curtail conflict by curbing the purchase of minerals illegally mined in areas controlled by these groups. NGOs such as Global Witness first and subsequently the United Nations, which established a Panel of Experts to document the links between armed conflict and natural resources, have successfully put the issue of conflict minerals on the international policy-making agenda with this kind of interpretation.[59] Monitoring the supply chain – 'traceability' in policy jargon – is perceived as a solution to many of eastern Congo's problems. The Enough Project[60] and Ben Affleck's Eastern Congo Initiative[61] (which are, again, good examples of celebrity-driven policy design) keep this reasoning alive.

Inspired by other traceability initiatives such as the 'no more blood diamonds' Kimberly Process,[62] the United States signed into law the Dodd–Frank Act in 2010.[63] Section 1502 of the Act requires companies listed on the US stock exchange to make sure that the products they manufacture or have contracted to manufacture do not contain minerals that directly or indirectly benefit armed groups in the DRC or in neighbouring countries. Taking action to end conflict was seen as being politically necessary, especially at a time when global demand boomed for high-tech devices built with the kinds of minerals coming out of the region. Advocates say that the legislation will help reduce violence in the region by depriving these groups of the profits they earn from conflict minerals.

Sceptics offer a more nuanced set of arguments and criticise Dodd–Frank for a number of compelling reasons. Because the standards it imposes on US businesses are expensive and compliance difficult to achieve, firms will be forced to find alternative sources for their minerals. One repercussion of this is its negative impact on millions of livelihoods. Miners and their families have indeed been victimised by a policy drawn up in the United States without adequate understanding of local dynamics or consultation with local stakeholders. This became apparent when President Kabila imposed a mining ban in the Kivus from September 2010 to March 2011, a decision that 'had a paralyzing effect on the regional economy and a dramatic impact on living conditions'.[64] Mantz argues that social structures have been broken by 'demonizing' artisanal mining.[65] Johnson contends that the ban had the exact opposite consequences to those intended. 'It is the absence of mining that fuels conflict' because it deprives the region of foreign earnings, removes economic opportunities, drives youth to earn money through violence and exacerbates competition over scarce resources among local stakeholders.[66] Drawing on the experience – and critiques – of Dodd–Frank, the European Commission and Parliament have announced plans to improve their mineral supply chain policy. Unlike Dodd–Frank, the European approach claims to recognise the need to take into account the root causes of conflict and state fragility and embed legislation in a broad regional development framework.[67] Canada has also introduced legislation requiring its companies to exercise due diligence in trading minerals from the Great Lakes Region.[68]

Regulation

Improving and modernising the regulatory framework is one of the most important priorities for Congolese mining – just as it is for all of the country's other natural resource sectors. After 32 years of Mobutu dictatorship, the subsequent absence of a coherent macroeconomic vision during Laurent-Désiré Kabila's reign, and his lack of transparency in awarding concessions, natural resource governance was in a shambles.[69] When Joseph Kabila became president after his father's assassination in January 2001, he re-established relations with donors who put Congo under tutelage during this abrupt father-to-son transition. Congo's sovereignty was circumscribed and controlled by international partners[70] who started to establish a series of important new policies in 2002.

A new mining law was approved, along with complementary and equally liberal laws regulating the forestry sector, investment and labour. This was one element of a comprehensive World Bank strategy to transform mining regulation all over Africa, based on the assumption that economic growth can best be achieved by attracting and facilitating foreign investment. The strategy's main mantras include transparency, efficiency, profitability, privatisation and investment security.[71] An important modification, compared with the previous mining law that dated back to 1981, was the end of the state monopoly in the mining sector. Also in the interest of attracting foreign private capital, there was a significant reduction in tax and customs fees.[72] The new mining law was accompanied by the drafting of a series of by-laws and the setting up of some specialised committees and departments within the Ministry of Mines.

The new law clearly placed the President of the Republic at the summit of the regulatory pyramid, institutionalising his power to take all important decisions relating to mining. The president has designed similar powers for himself in the oil sector. The other key administrative entities are the Ministry of Mines (responsible for awarding and revoking concessions), provincial governors, the Mining Cadastre (a licensing system that tracks who is doing what and where), the Mining Inspectorate (in charge of monitoring security, health, labour, production, transportation and social issues), the Environmental Protection Inspectorate, and a quality-control agency to make sure that certificates correspond to the minerals and grades specified. The Ministry of Finance collects tax and customs revenues through its specialist offices.[73] The establishment of these bodies is a necessary start, but one that needs time to move towards real implementation. Ambitious and usually confident, the World Bank accepted the necessity of reforming the sector with a long-term vision, recognising that it 'will not be easy and there are likely to be plenty of hurdles along the way'.[74] Reform of the mining sector and comprehensive reform of the state are indeed interdependent.

The negotiation process that aimed to reform the sector was sensitive because mining is an extremely high-stakes business controlled by politically well-connected factions (mainly Katangese) that function to accommodate their own non-transparent agendas. Augustin Katumba Mwanke, Joseph Kabila's *éminence grise* (until he died in a plane crash in 2012), was the undisputed kingpin in the Congolese mining sector. He was probably the only person who had an overview of it. In addition to having outstanding political finesse, Katumba had learned the mining business in South Africa after having studied at the Polytechnic Faculty at the University of Kinshasa. A controversial tycoon, Dan Gertler, has emerged as one of the most important private investors in the DRC. A close associate of Katumba prior to his death, Gertler is widely rumoured to be the Kabila family financier.

The 2002 mining law was intended to improve governance and thus increase stimulus for international investment by transforming the involvement of the state, which saw its role as mining operator decrease and evolve into one with increased responsibility for administrative facilitation and oversight. The state, according to this logic, is supposed to regulate, not operate as a mining actor. The World Bank was categorical in its assessment that the state-owned mining enterprises were inefficient. 'Privatisation' is the term most frequently used to describe the process but it is not entirely accurate because the former state monopoly companies became 'private' companies with the state owning all or the majority of the shares. The setting up of joint ventures was a common form of ownership transfer. The dismantling of Gécamines is the obvious example, but the same logic applied to the Société Minière de Kilo-Moto (acquired by the South African giant AngloGold Ashanti) and MIBA, in which the pan-African group Mwana Africa has a 20 per cent interest. Gécamines' 'privatisation' was accompanied by a socially aggressive staff reduction of 10,000 workers funded by the World Bank.[75] The ore deposits of this former giant, along with its very largely dilapidated stock of equipment and infrastructure, were made available to private investors under a new joint venture regime whose bids were evaluated according to financial, environmental, social, legal and technical criteria. Some concessions were granted to international corporations with a due diligence discourse but others were not. This situation has contributed to ongoing uncertainty over who the real actors are. Joseph Kabila accepted the privatisation programme because he was clearly able to benefit from it. Some of the deposits ended up in the hands of Chinese operators about whom little information is available. The World Bank strategy backfired to a large extent because the Kabila entourage became the private shareholders in some of the richest and most accessible deposits. Instead of depoliticising the mining sector, the Bank's strategy reinforced the Kabila family's capacity to access and control mineral wealth.[76]

Another initiative to improve mining governance was the mining review launched in 2007. This was also motivated by the need to clarify the concessions signed first by Laurent-Désiré Kabila and then by Joseph Kabila. Sixty-one mining licences were reviewed; 43 contracts were approved and 17 rejected in 2009. However, the revision process was controversial and suffered from some predictable shortcomings. The government lacked the capacity to understand the legal and technical complexity of the contracts. Most importantly, there was a lack of political will to use the revision process as a real management strategy.

Again, the outcome was a redistribution of benefits to companies with connections to the political elite. It is widely believed that bribes were paid for those contracts that were approved because a well-conducted review would have resulted in a much higher rejection rate.

Efforts to clean up the mining sector have met with only limited success because even the best technical reform strategies cannot be effective in the current political landscape. Two examples testify to an unrelenting lack of transparency and corruption. In September 2007, Congo and China signed a two-phase loan agreement amounting to nearly $10 billion. The agreement (with annexes), brokered by the secretive Katumba Mwanke, is a mere nine pages! In the first phase, $6.5 billion were earmarked for infrastructure and development; the second phase is a $3.2 billion loan for the modernisation of mining infrastructure. In exchange for the loan, China receives rights to mine 8 million tonnes of copper, 200,000 tonnes of cobalt and 372 tonnes of gold.[77] Guaranteed by the Congolese government, this would exonerate China from paying taxes and duties for a 30-year period. But little is known about the fundamental terms of the deal, including information about the pricing of minerals, what specific infrastructure projects are planned (and at what cost) and, finally, at what rate profits are to be taxed.[78] Congolese opponents perceived the deal as a sell-out of the country's natural resources, suspecting that it was a ruse to veil the political elites' scheme to grab money at the expense of ordinary Congolese – while allowing China to reap disproportionate profits. Europe and the United States disapproved of the deal because of the absence of conditionalities, such as respect for human rights and the environment, good governance and due diligence.[79] The International Monetary Fund and the World Bank opposed it because they saw it as a source of renewed indebtedness that the Congo would not be able to absorb. The controversial infrastructure-for-minerals deal was consequently downsized, putting the $3 billion infrastructure phase on hold and removing the government's guarantee on the mining project.

A second example of non-transparency was the 2011 sell-off of state assets to fund President Kabila's electoral campaign. The UK member of parliament Eric Joyce exposed 'a systematic pattern of underselling Congolese mining assets to off-shore "shell" companies ... the ultimate beneficial owners of which are often unknown, with the result that the Congolese people do not benefit from the vast mineral wealth in their country'.[80] He calculated a loss of $5.5 billion to the country. The mechanism was rather simple: the president sold state assets at discounted prices to companies registered in the British Virgin Islands. The companies, many of which were associated with Dan Gertler, sold them to multinational firms, earning significant windfall profits. According to Joyce, 'these transactions were not disclosed by the DRC government. None of these asset sales were put out to public tender.'[81]

Joyce's damning report was confirmed by the prestigious Africa Progress Panel, which, in a similar battery of charges, reported a $1.36 billion loss in revenues between 2010 and 2012 from the under-pricing of mining assets sold to offshore companies.[82] The government made grandiloquent declarations about the need for transparency in the sale of state assets in 2010 and 2011 and passed a series of ad hoc measures. As nothing concrete resulted from these promises, the International Monetary Fund, the African Development Bank and the World Bank all sanctioned Kinshasa by suspending loan programmes. The panel's assessment, which points to the long-term engagement needed before change will come, also highlighted that 'the complex structures of interlocking offshore companies, commercial secrecy on the part of major mining companies, and limited reporting by state companies and government agencies to the DRC's legislators, creates what amounts to a secret world – a world in which vast fortunes appear to be accumulated at the expense of the DRC's people'.[83]

A slightly more positive counter-example to secrecy and reform failure is the DRC's reconnection with the Extractive Industries Transparency Initiative (EITI)[84] as a full member in 2014 after having been suspended the year before. The decision, however, was probably motivated more as a policy encouragement than as a result of improvement backed up by objectively verifiable technical criteria. EITI seeks to promote transparent and accountable management of natural resources to ensure that they benefit ordinary people and not only corrupt elites. It is based on a sophisticated accounting and auditing system whereby oil, gas and mining companies disclose the taxes they pay to the national governments in the countries where they have activities, which in turn make that information public. The links in its value chain approach include access to resources, monitoring, tax collection, revenue allocation and distribution of revenues for sustainable projects. Ensuring that the Congolese government had the necessary computing systems and expertise was an important step in reaching EITI compliance status. EITI is part of the Publish What You Pay international coalition of NGOs that campaigns for the mandatory disclosure of company payments and government revenues from the oil, gas, and mining sector as well as the public disclosure of extractive industry contracts and licensing procedures.[85]

Growth with Governance in the Mineral Sector (PROMINES) is a project that shares EITI's objectives. Committed to the need to improve the regulatory framework, the World Bank established it and funds it along with the United Kingdom's Department for International Development.[86] It is designed to strengthen the capacity of Congolese institutions to manage the mining sector, enhance investment conditions and revenues from mining by improving access to up-to-date geological datasets, and help increase socioeconomic benefits while contributing to sustainable development. Improved tax collection and reporting are a particularly important PROMINES priority. These are all ambitious goals because the political culture of secrecy adhered to by mining companies and by the Congolese elites is a constant threat to both EITI and PROMINES.[87]

As in other natural resource sectors, such as forestry, oil and hydroelectric power, mitigating negative social and environmental impacts is one of the clearly stated objectives of the mining reform process. Nevertheless, a wide range of problems persist. A United Nations Environment Programme report identified landscape degradation, water and air pollution and radioactive contamination as environmental problems caused by large-scale industrial mining. The report could have added that thousands of *creuseurs* digging holes randomly in the search for ores have a greater impact on the landscape and nature than a large-scale open-pit mine. Mercury contamination (mercury is used in gold mining), human health hazards, forest and biodiversity degradation and human rights abuses (such as child labour and prostitution) are some of the negative consequences of small-scale mining.[88] There is also a high level of exposure to cobalt among people living in Katanga, resulting from consumption of contaminated leafy green vegetables.[89] Water pollution from industrial-scale ore processing and refining, with its negative repercussions on food security (pollution also affects livestock and fish), public health and livelihoods, has been targeted by some NGOs as a violation of the human right to water.[90] Although not alone, Chinese mining companies have a particularly poor record in environmental compliance.[91] In addition to being complacent about the violations of mining companies, the government and ad hoc regulatory bodies simply do not have the means to carry out adequate social and environmental impact assessments, especially in the informal and artisanal mining sectors.

An emerging renaissance

Despite the sluggishness of the institutional reform process, private investments in industrial mining have been surging. The early years of the Joseph Kabila presidency were marked by a shift from the dominance of exploration by junior companies to the gradual arrival of the majors. Since 2005, production has risen and state revenues have increased steadily. Mining has been the main driver of the country's more than 8 per cent growth rate in the past few years.

Most companies reporting exports over the past few years are still in the exploration and set-up phases, exporting minerals purchased for the most part from artisanal miners.[92] This is particularly the case for the '3Ts' but is less applicable to cobalt and copper, although some companies combine products mined industrially and with those dug by *creuseurs*, whose production costs are lower. As companies now enter the production phase, there is a strong likelihood that revenues paid into the national treasury will continue to increase. The period of tax exemption status for many of these companies is coming to an end, which should also augment state revenues. In an annual survey that assesses how mineral endowments and public policy factors such as taxation and regulatory uncertainty affect exploration investment, the DRC was ranked 62 out of 122.[93] This ranking is somewhat better than those produced by many human development and democracy watchdogs.

The constantly shifting play of mergers, acquisitions and titles changing owners makes it difficult to establish a clear overview of who all the real mining actors are. It is nevertheless possible to identify some of the big investors and producers. The EITI lists eight state-owned mining companies and 31 joint ventures and presents an incomplete inventory of 93 private mining companies.[94] The objective of this section is to provide some insight into the main actors today, but it does not aim to present an exhaustive inventory. Identifying some of these actors helps put the mining sector's challenges and opportunities into perspective, while clearly revealing the unpredictable and globalised nature of Congolese mining.

Freeport-McMoRan Inc., a leading international natural resources company with headquarters in Arizona, is mining's biggest player in Congo today. It is the majority owner (56 per cent) of the Tenke Fungurume mine along with Canada's Lundin Mining Corporation (24 per cent) and Gécamines (20 per cent). Freeport is in a $2 billion investment phase.[95] Before the company is able to produce copper and generate revenues, staff have to be recruited and trained, and factories, power plants and related infrastructure need to be built. Katanga's Tenke Fungurume mine is a major copper and cobalt deposit that has changed hands frequently over the past decades. It was formerly held by Phelps Dodge until that company was taken over by Freeport in 2009 in a $26 billion acquisition.[96] At the time, Tenke was considered to be the world's largest undeveloped copper and cobalt mine. Maurice Tempelsman, a Belgian-American businessman and diamond merchant, put together a consortium of international mining partners in the then named Société Minière de Tenke Fungurume in the early 1970s. The project was aborted, however, due to the fall in world copper prices and delays in the construction of the Inga–Shaba electricity transmission line. Tempelsman, a discreet associate of President Mobutu, was more famous as the long-time companion of former American first lady Jacqueline Kennedy Onassis.

One of the world's largest companies and the biggest trader of metals and minerals, the Anglo-Swiss Glencore, operates the prized Kansuki and Mutanda mines in the southern Katanga copperbelt. Glencore was founded by the controversial Belgian-born international fugitive Marc Rich, whom *The Economist* once described as 'the king of commodities'.[97] Dan Gertler facilitated Glencore's entry into mining in Congo according to Global Witness, which has called attention to the secrecy surrounding its acquisition conditions.[98] The two mines are slated to boost Congo's copper production and could produce a staggering 40 per cent of the world's cobalt.

Katanga Mining Limited (of which Glencore controls 75 per cent) is another big copper and cobalt player. Officially registered in Switzerland, it appears as a complicated holding with partners and subsidiaries based in Canada, the British Virgin Islands and South Africa. Its corporate history is one of multiple mergers, takeovers and joint ventures. It exploits the rich underground Kamoto mine, which until its literal collapse in 1990 produced 3 million tonnes of ore per year.[99] After an expensive and lengthy rehabilitation process, Kamoto copper ore production climbed to nearly 2 million tonnes in 2014.[100] Highlighting the ups and downs of the business, the owners of the mine announced in September 2015 that they were suspending production of copper and cobalt due to weak commodity prices.[101]

Banro, a Canadian company, mines gold along the Twangiza–Namoya gold belt in South Kivu and Maniema. Its production target is 100,000 ounces of gold per year. Banro also holds permits for the Kamituga and Lugushwa concessions. The company has encountered financial problems, however; world gold prices are volatile and have been falling, production has not met expected forecasts, and access to bond markets is declining.[102]

Mining Company Katanga (MCK) is a noteworthy example of how politics and mining can be mutually beneficial. The company was founded by an outstanding businessman and politician. After having amassed a huge personal fortune through business and mining, Moïse Katumbi was elected governor of Katanga in 2007. He had been recruited by Katumba Mwanke in 2006 to campaign in Katanga for Joseph Kabila in the presidential elections. MCK was a joint venture partner of the Canadian junior company Anvil Mining (which was subsequently purchased in 2012 by the Chinese MMG). An intuitive populist with a staff of competent technocrats, Katumbi was a much respected governor until he stepped down in March 2015, using his personal fortune to maintain development momentum in his province. This development, however, is hampered by the non-compliance of the central government to transfer 40 per cent of tax revenues back to the provinces where those revenues were generated. This problem also accounts for why many Katangese – who supported Kabila in the previous two presidential elections – have been withdrawing support for him in the run-up to the 2016 poll. Ownership of the champion football team T. P. Mazembe has reinforced Katumbi's charisma.

Greater investment in exploration is a prerequisite for the successful renaissance of the sector. However, budgets allocated to this fundamental operation are low for the moment. In 2014, they amounted to $306 million, which is quite insignificant given the need for updated data about ore deposits.[103] The global market moves rapidly so Congo needs to continue exploration. The element europium offers an interesting example.[104] Because of its increasing use in the electronics industry (mainly for lighting and display systems – including for television and computer screens), the United States and the European Union have classified europium as a critical material – and investors are prospecting for it. This mineral could be an important global commodity in the not-too-distant future – perhaps something like coltan was in the 1980s.

The recent discovery of the very rich Kamoa copper deposit near Kolwezi in Katanga, now held by Ivanhoe Mines, also proves the commercial usefulness of investing in exploration.[105] Exploratory drilling took place there as recently as 2008 and its discovery is a real bonanza for its owners. Ivanhoe's billionaire chief executive Robert Friedland, who bought the company from Dan Gertler in 2011,[106] was incidentally Steve Jobs' college mentor in 1972.[107] China's Zijin Mining is negotiating with Ivanhoe to purchase a 49.5 per cent stake in Kamoa (where production is scheduled to begin by the end of 2018) but the deal is currently being blocked by the DRC government, which is also trying to increase its own ownership in the mine.[108]

Conclusion: future prospects

The emerging renaissance in Congo's mining sector is fragile and its future momentum is uncertain. With the necessary energy, copper production – which was around 1 million tonnes in 2015[109] – could reach 1.2 million tonnes by 2020.[110] Improving the availability of energy is particularly important in the refining phases, which provide much more added value than merely exporting unprocessed ore. The dependency of mining productivity on energy is an obvious example of the need to develop Congo's productive industries in an integrated way. Mining is forecast to generate revenues equivalent to between 15 per cent and 20 per cent of GDP by 2020,[111] which could translate into sound macroeconomic results including growth, low inflation, an acceptable trade balance and a stable Congolese franc. Production and resource potential in this respect is being achieved. There is even increasing evidence of an emerging middle class related to mining in some parts of the DRC, notably in Katanga.

Perspectives for ordinary Congolese, however, remain precarious. They continue to struggle with unemployment, food insecurity, poor public service provision, tense relations with political institutions and all of the other indicators that keep them low on the United Nation's Human Development Index. Will people derive some benefit from Congo's non-renewable mineral wealth before it runs out? Much more needs to be achieved in terms of management and governance before an affirmative response to this question is possible. This begs another question: when will these resources be depleted? The answer is problematic: nobody knows at the moment because the exact geological potential is not adequately documented. Hence, there can be no long-term macroeconomic forecasting.

The regulatory framework put in place in 2002 was an important start but it needs to be revised and updated. Should artisanal and small-scale mining be more formalised? If so, what kind of legislation and monitoring could realistically increase state revenues?[112] Stakeholders from the private sector and government recognise the pertinence of revising the mining law but how can very different expectations be reconciled? One controversial fiscal proposition is increasing mandatory state participation from the current 5 per cent to 35 per cent, which private investors oppose. It was important to attract investors with liberal tax incentives, but how does this benefit the average Congolese citizen? The World Bank was the real driver behind the reform process – in mining as in other sectors – but its future capacity to influence policy is also limited and uncertain. Mobutu cleverly sabotaged World Bank policies and Laurent-Désiré Kabila broke ties with the Bretton Woods institutions. Given constantly shifting global dynamics in the sector and Joseph Kabila's political opportunism, there is no reason to assume that the World Bank will continue to be able to influence the design of the regulatory framework – and even less its implementation. China has become a major international actor in the copper business in the DRC, which puts President Kabila in a strong bargaining position because China's engagement weakens Western governments' efforts to enforce policies of good governance and due diligence.

The fragile mining renaissance also depends on fundamental priorities that lie well beyond the sector itself. There can be no sustained development of the sector without improved relations with Angola and Uganda – and especially with Rwanda. There can be no sustained development without significant state reform, including implementation of fiscal decentralisation and vigorous investment in infrastructure and energy.[113] It also depends on the cooperation of a committed and efficient cadre of civil servants responsible for mining, the environment, labour and tax collection. The extremely liberal investment conditions designed by the Bretton Woods institutions could be interpreted as reducing state revenues that could be invested in local development, which partly explains why some Congolese officials are calling for the revision of the regulatory framework. The biggest challenge remains the permanency of entrenched patrimonial control of mineral wealth. Competent international technocrats can help reform the state, but past experiences have shown that they often lack an understanding of Congolese political culture. Officials in government and the civil service seem always to be one step ahead of the regulatory measures aimed at improving transparency and accountability. Private companies are complicit with Congolese elite networks, as witnessed by their exploitation of complex corporate structures, non-transparent accounting practices and strategically orchestrated merger and acquisition cabals. The fact that there is so much suspicion and so little real information about ownership of mining companies is just one of many challenges.

Chapter 7

CONCLUSION: UNCERTAINTY AND PREDATION IN A LAND OF PLENTY

The destinies of Congo and the world will continue to be tightly intertwined because of the country's amazing natural resource base. The supply of minerals for high-tech industries and Congo's uncertain role in mitigating – or contributing to – climate change are two remarkable examples of this intertwining. The previous chapters, which presented the country's resource potential in a cautiously prescient way, each offered balanced assessments of both that potential and its associated challenges, emphasising the complexity of natural resource governance. The message that they convey should now be clear: Congo's natural resources offer tremendous promise for the country's development – and that of its people – but positive change is hampered by serious problems and many constraints. That is the crux of *Congo's Environmental Paradox*. For many valid reasons, therefore, optimistic thinking about this natural resource powerhouse appears far less frequently than the litany of blunt critiques and caveats. Nevertheless, the evidence from all of the resource sectors points to new patterns of transformation and opportunities.

The political economy of Congo's natural resource sectors is characterised by considerable uncertainty, which makes it difficult to decipher the real meaning and implications of these patterns. This book, however, should contribute to looking at them in a new light, especially because of its emphasis on an interconnected and integrated approach. Many communities in central Africa have an expression for interdependency: the hand has five digits, each one different but all necessary to make the hand a hand. Forests, land, water, oil and minerals are analogous to that hand – five facets of the environment making Congo what it is. Interconnectedness in this context refers to the relationships between the resource sectors themselves but also the links between local Congolese realities and global dynamics. The evidence should also allow readers to grasp the incredible value of these resources for a wide range of stakeholders. These include ordinary Congolese and the government, foreign investors and local workers, formal and informal actors, people living off the land and those who thrive at deal making. As there is innovation in all of these overlapping relationships, changing realities need to be reflected in new analytical discourses.

Ostensible achievements cannot disguise the challenges analysed sector by sector, some of which are structural. Physically reuniting Congo's fragmented territory and rehabilitating the country's dilapidated infrastructure are absolute prerequisites for improved and modernised natural resource management. Development in mining, oil production, industrial logging and agriculture is hobbled by insufficient transport infrastructure. Without the infrastructure needed to enable the mobility of people and resources, there will be no development. Energy shortages will continue to jeopardise the entire economic life of the country for the foreseeable future while also putting tremendous pressure on households and the environment. Without power, the transformation of copper and cobalt creates wealth outside the DRC, not within it. Consequently, other countries develop to the detriment of the DRC, whose international competitiveness is put on hold.

Others challenges are institutional. *Congo's Environmental Paradox* points to weaknesses in the legal and regulatory frameworks. These have evolved over the past decade, harmonising with international norms and monitoring concerns, but revisions and further reforms are still badly needed – especially ones that could facilitate effective control by honest watchdog institutions and real application by the Congolese government, with the cooperation of its international partners. Political and institutional dysfunction, predation in the public administration sector and the inability of the government to guarantee security or law and order have far-reaching implications that limit the country's options for capitalising on its natural resource potential. All of the chapters have identified crippling governance shortcomings, policy absurdities and predatory practices. Although it is not totally unrealistic to assume that governance systems have the potential to be reformed at some point, there are only limited signs of a willingness to implement such changes today.

Challenges also result from the social and cultural contexts. Demographic growth and urbanisation put pressure on water resources and redefine land use priorities, while competition is intensifying between forest conservation and farming. There are more and more people who depend on a finite and deteriorating resource base, a problem potentially aggravated by land-grabbing initiatives. Without formal sector employment, people consider the exploitation of natural resources to feed their families as both a right and a necessity. This is felt strongly, especially in rural areas where populations have limited livelihood options. Popular beliefs can sometimes be very damaging to the environment: the perception that fish spawn from grains of sand and that the forests will always be full of bushmeat because wildlife is a gift of God are striking examples.

The absence of consensual land use plans at the national and local level is another threat to natural resource management. Mining – and increasingly oil – supersedes other land use allocations because of current and expected revenues from licensing, exploitation and taxation. Oil exploration in the Virunga National Park by SOCO, mining concessions that overlap protected areas and forest concessions, and arbitrary decisions made about agricultural space are all specific problems identified in the previous chapters. This unresolved ambiguity over legality and legitimacy fuels competing claims to space and resources and in turn leads to unsustainable resource management policies and practices. Uncertainty over land ownership also leads to wider conflict. According to the government, land belongs to the state. People living in rural communities, however, consider themselves to be the true landowners, based on ancestral rights.

The involvement of international partners in resource management has produced unsatisfactory results in the different sectors. Lack of coordination, competing development strategies and ideologies (exacerbated by hidden diplomatic agendas), a misunderstanding of local realities and short-term visions are some of the reasons why cooperation policies have been flawed. They help explain why there are so few meaningful natural resource management success stories designed and implemented by Congo's technical and financial partners. Successful projects do exist, of course, but they tend to be isolated cases in a donor-driven patchwork where national ownership is minimal, making natural resource potential a chimera. Without Congolese engagement, outside actors are powerless to fully capitalise on the country's potential or work effectively.

Western environmental non-governmental organisations (NGOs) have been helpful in assisting the Ministry of Environment in managing protected areas but they have not contributed to solving fundamental problems relating to perceptions of sovereignty and legitimacy, for example. The World Bank-inspired privatisation of state-owned mining companies contributed to regime entrenchment, as President Kabila and his business partners bought up shares in profitable concessions, mainly through companies registered in foreign tax havens. Large multinational corporations, regional consortia and the world's most powerful financial institutions have not yet succeeded in putting together an investment package for the Inga hydroelectric site. It is too early to say whether or not the Chinese resources-for-infrastructure model will provide sustainable benefits to the Congolese people, but it is unlikely to be the truly win–win solution it is promoted to be. Western development agencies and NGOs have contributed to empowering agricultural communities, but without roads and commercialisation incentives, these efforts at empowerment have only limited impact.

Predation is undeniably the overarching threat to improved natural resource management. It takes many forms at many different levels, and it emanates from within the DRC and from beyond the country's borders. Appropriation of public resources by privileged political and economic groups for their own benefit is a longstanding and enduring system in the DRC. In the heyday of the Mobutu kleptocracy, Western development workers had a favourite story, one that was also told sardonically by ordinary people. God and Saint Peter were busy divvying up wealth across the world. As the Lord appeared overly generous with Zaire, Saint Peter remarked that the country seemed to be getting too much, compared with some that received little. The Lord responded to Saint Peter: 'I know what I'm doing; I'll fill the land with Zairians to balance things out.' This anecdote was primarily voiced as a commentary on Mobutu-style patrimonialism: those in power simply could not be trusted to manage the country's resources.

Then and now, ruling elites cynically steal as much as they can – as quickly as they can – with no apparent concern for the population nor any commitment to implement a development agenda, which is currently non-existent. Rule by thieves, kleptocracy and *Raub-wirtschaft* are some of the terms applied to Congo's – and previously Zaire's – predatory political economy. But foreign actors, some of whom still view Congo as offering a natural resource get-rich-quick bonanza, continue to be complicit with Congolese authorities in their rapacious schemes. The involvement of foreign actors in resource pillaging, from King Leopold II and Belgian concessionary companies during colonial rule to global multinationals today, is a constant pattern that continues to undermine natural resource development for the broader benefit of the Congolese people. This is not to say that all forms of foreign investment are necessarily bad. On the contrary – foreign direct investment is needed to provide jobs, services and revenues. Some foreign companies respect their fiscal obligations to the state, exercise corporate social and environmental responsibilities and adhere to due diligence recommendations. Nonetheless, even when they do, they have little say in how the government uses revenues.

Because the Congolese state is weak and largely ineffective, it has difficulty in securing its territory and asserting its sovereignty. It is therefore unable to fully cope with pressures from regional predators. The illegal exploitation of natural resources (mainly minerals and timber) by Rwanda and Uganda are the most flagrant examples. But as the previous chapters have indicated, the DRC has poor relations with most of its neighbours, which with varying degrees of legality are also taking advantage of Congolese resources. Angola derives significant benefits from the extraction of Congolese oil. The Lord's Resistance Army and organised crime syndicates, linked to Chinese buyers, are complicit with South Sudanese poachers in the Garamba National Park. The use of cross-border water resources is a cause of current and potential regional conflicts.

Poor governance appears to be a fairly easy target when accounting for the underdevelopment of Congo's natural resource sectors. But given the combined negative impacts of these structural, cultural and political factors, even in the event of regime change it is unlikely that the Congolese government will be willing or able to reform natural resource management practices to any significant extent. While improved governance is necessary, it is not enough. Even in a hypothetical future when the Congolese people have the opportunity to elect a president committed to a democratically motivated development agenda, these factors will handicap improved natural resource management for a long time to come. Resolving these problems will necessitate the commitment of powerful actors with competing claims and interests.

Change therefore also needs to be understood by looking at the role of non-state – and foreign – actors. Of course, poor governance matters but its impact varies according to sector and activity. Many natural resource management changes seem to take place beyond the state's reach. Good or bad governance has limited impact on production in the oil economy, although it does affect the way in which profits are redistributed. Big mining companies have integrated poor governance risks into their business plans, while informal economic actors – artisanal miners and loggers, for example – have had time to design strategies to operate despite, and more often than not because of, state failure. More democratic institutions that adhere to a development agenda could help farmers, but poor governance provides little incentive to them to improve production and post-harvest techniques or to increase the proportion of crops that go to market. As the Chinese assess investment options in major infrastructure development projects, the role of the Kinshasa government is probably only a secondary consideration.

The starting point of this book was the hypothesis that Congo's natural resources have the potential to contribute to development. The findings provided in the chapters timidly confirm that hypothesis, indicating that it is not so much a question of *if* they will contribute but rather *when* they will do so. However, *when* is uncertain and also appears to be a long way off. Given the complexities within and across the different sectors, it is difficult to identify what exactly is required for this contribution to development to occur. Embedding natural resource management far deeper within broader, efficient and realistic state-building initiatives is undoubtedly the most important condition for this to happen.

NOTES

Chapter 1

1   Cleaver (2012).
2   'Moody's assigns B3 ratings to the Democratic Republic of the Congo, stable outlook', Moody's Investors Service, 6 September 2013. Available at www.moodys.com/research/Moodys-assigns-B3-ratings-to-the-Democratic-Republic-of-the--PR_281558?WT.mc_id=NLTITLE_YYYYMMDD_PR_281558.
3   'Sub-Saharan Africa implements the most business regulatory reforms worldwide', World Bank press release, 29 October 2014. Available at www.worldbank.org/en/news/press-release/2014/10/29/sub-saharan-africa-business-regulatory-reforms-worldwide.
4   Trefon (2011a: 118–19).
5   President Kabila's failed bid to amend the Constitution to allow for a third term as president in January 2015 is a good example of the growing strength of the political opposition, as is the splintering of the presidential majority in September 2015.
6   See http://devinit.org/wp-content/uploads/2013/09/Investments-to-End-Poverty-Chapter-10-Congo-Dem-Rep.pdf.
7   Englebert (2014).
8   Roxburgh *et al.* (2010).
9   'International Human Development Indicators', United Nations Development Programme. Available at http://hdr.undp.org/en/countries.
10 For an overview of these issues for Africa in general, see Young (2012) and van Beck (2011).
11 Trefon (2004; 2011a); Trefon with Ngoy (2007).
12 Herderschee *et al.* (2012) have made a somewhat similar attempt, but without focusing specifically on natural resources.
13 Jewsiewicki (1979); see also Buelens and Marysse (2009).
14 Hanson *et al.* (2014).
15 For an early discussion of the integrated management approach of tropical forests in Africa, see Maldague *et al.* (1997); for a more recent assessment see Achu Samndong and Nhantumbo (2015).

Chapter 2

1   'La RDC réclame 21 milliards de $', BBC Afrique, 19 August 2015. Available at www.bbc.com/afrique/region/2015/08/150819_rdc.

2   Stanley (1878).

3   Vansina (1990: 39–46).

4   Debroux *et al.* (2007: 10); Counsell (2006: 8).

5   Debroux *et al.* (2007: 1).

6   Eba'a Atyi and Bayol (2009: 122).

7   Billand (2012: 66).

8   Doumenge (1990: 23).

9   *Ibid.*: 20.

10 'Tanzania: tourism earns more revenue than gold', *Arusha Times*, 4 April 2015. Available at http://allafrica.com/stories/201504061246.html.

11 Delegation of the European Commission (2006).

12 Eba'a Atyi and Bayol (2009: 123).

13 Trefon and Kabuyaya (2009).

14 Misser (2013a: 12).

15 Colom Bickford (2016).

16 'Howard Buffett bets on hydropower to rebuild eastern Congo', Reuters, 20 August 2015. Available at www.reuters.com/article/2015/08/20/us-congo democratic-buffett-idUSKCN0QP13V20150820.

17 'Addressing climate change in the Democratic Republic of Congo: support for training and reforestation', Global Climate Change Alliance. Available at www. gcca.eu/national-programmes/africa/gcca-democratic-republic-of-congo.

18 Ernst *et al.* (2012: 32).

19 *Ibid.*: 33.

20 Zhou *et al.* (2014).

21 Ernst *et al.* (2013).

22 Geist and Lambin (2002).

23 Fairhead and Leach (1998: xiv).

24 Marien (2009: 211).

25 Trefon *et al.* (2010).

26 Schure *et al.* (2013: 34).

27 Eba'a Atyi and Bayol (2009: 111).

28 Schure *et al.* (2013: 36).

29 *Ibid.*: 34.

30 Trefon with Ngoy (2007: 47–53).

31 Counsell (2006: 10).

32 Wilkie *et al.* (1998).

33 Trefon (2006).

34 Greenpeace (2012).

35   Eba'a Atyi and Bayol (2009: 117).
36   Bayol *et al.* (2012: 43).
37   Resource Extraction Monitoring (2013: 4).
38   Megevand *et al.* (2013: 40).
39   Lescuyer *et al.* (2012: 103); Chevallier and du Preez (2012).
40   Lescuyer *et al.* (2012: 97).
41   Debroux *et al.* (2007: 7).
42   The European Commission has nevertheless funded the Centre for International Forestry Research to examine the possibilities of integrating informal domestic timber markets into the national legal framework. For information about the Pro-Formal project, see www.cifor.org/pro-formal/home.html.
43   Bisschop (2012: 2).
44   United Nations Panel of Inquiry (2003; 2009). For a more analytical source, see Clark (2002).
45   Shambaugh *et al.* (2001: 16).
46   'President Bush's Initiative Against Illegal Logging', The White House. Available at http://georgewbush-whitehouse.archives.gov/infocus/illegal-logging/.
47   'FLEGT Voluntary Partnership Agreements (VPAs)', European Commission. Available at http://ec.europa.eu/environment/forests/flegt.htm.
48   See http://ic.fsc.org/.
49   See http://rem.org.uk/.
50   FERN and Forest Peoples Programme (2014).
51   Hoare (2007: 22).
52   Information in this paragraph comes from correspondence with Ministry of Environment staff.
53   Vermeulen (2014); Eba'a Atyi and Bayol (2009).
54   Resource Extraction Monitoring (2011: 13)
55   Javelle and Veit (2012).
56   Interview with Member of Parliament, Kinshasa, March 2014.
57   Two examples are Avocats Verts and Océan.
58   Reed *et al.* (2015: 42).
59   Stern (2006).
60   Commission on Climate and Tropical Forests (2009: 20).
61   Wunder (2005).
62   Credit Suisse *et al.* (2014).
63   Ribot and Larson (2012).
64   Kipalu and Mukungu (2013).
65   Kearsley *et al.* (2013).
66   Karsenty (2012).
67   République Démocratique du Congo (2013a).
68   FERN and Forest Peoples Programme (2014).

69 PwC (2012: 4).

70 Mpoyi (2012).

71 Brown (2013).

Chapter 3

1   Ntoto and Lunze (2013: 2).

2   Hochschild (1998).

3   Demunter (1975: 235–7).

4   Mokili Danga Kassa (1998: 567–8); Le Plae (1939).

5   Chausse *et al.* (2012: 93).

6   See Global Food Security Index at http://foodsecurityindex.eiu.com/ Country.

7   UNDP (2013: 169).

8   Tollens (2004a: 1).

9   Poulton (2012).

10 Chausse *et al.* (2012: 2).

11 Jansson *et al.* (2009).

12 Mastaki Namegabe (2006: 58).

13 Vansina (1990: 255).

14 Huart and Tombu (2010: 90).

15 Bezy *et al.* (1981: 117–18).

16 Mokili Danga Kassa (1998: 324).

17 Young and Turner (1985: 179).

18 Mokili Danga Kassa (1998: 326–7).

19 Ndaywel è Nziem (1998: 705).

20 The DRC has around only 20 agricultural economists according to Belgian-trained Roger Ntoto, Professor of Agricultural Economy at the University of Kinshasa. Interview, Kinshasa, January 2014.

21 Trefon (2011a: 55–9).

22 République Démocratique du Congo (2013b: 3).

23 'Création des parcs agro-industriels: des Américains d'accord avec Matata Ponyo', *Le Phare*, 20 January 2014. Available at www.lephareonline.net/ creation-des-parcs-agro-industriels-des-americains-daccord-avec-matata-ponyo/.

24 The 2003 Maputo Declaration is a commitment by African governments to devote at least 10 per cent of national budgets to agriculture. Only 7 out of 53 governments have done so.

25 Huart *et al.* (2013).

26 Deborah Bryceson's research is particularly noteworthy on this topic. She has a webpage devoted specifically to her relevant publications about de-agrarianisation at www.bryceson.net/Deagrarianization_%26_Mining.html.

27 Rackley (2006); Tollens (2004b).

28 Trefon (2011b).

29 Bryceson (2006: 4).

30 Some of Kinshasa's main markets are Marché Central, Liberté, Gambela, Matete, Simba Zigida, UPN and Rond-Point Ngaba.

31 Banchirigah and Hilson (2010).

32 Bezy *et al.* (1981: 150).

33 Jackson (2002: 528).

34 *Ibid.*: 529.

35 '2015 UNHCR country operations profile: Democratic Republic of the Congo', Office of the United Nations High Commissioner for Refugees. Available at www.unhcr.org/pages/49e45c366.html.

36 Heyse (1940).

37 Roberts (1979); Leitenberg (1981).

38 Leitenberg (1981: 116).

39 Le Roy (1991: 21).

40 Anseeuw (2013: 173).

41 For more on Feronia's DRC investments, see GRAIN and RIAO-RDC (2015).

42 Bräutigam and Haisen Zhang (2013: 1686).

43 'Congo's secret sales', Global Witness, 13 May 2014. Available at www. globalwitness.org/library/secret-sales.

44 Sassen (2013: 29).

45 GRAIN (2013: 5).

46 *Ibid.*

47 Cheru and Modi (2013: 4).

48 Matondi *et al.* (2011: 194).

49 See www.iea.org/topics/renewables/subtopics/bioenergy/.

50 Cotula (2013: 72).

51 Interview with Hervé Kimoni, student at ERAIFT (École Régionale Post-universitaire d'Aménagement et de Gestion Intégrés des Forêts et Territoires Tropicaux), Luki, March 2015.

52 Tollens (2004b).

53 Bisiaux *et al.* (2009: 30).

54 Cleaver and Schreiber (1994: 144).

55 Karsenty (2010: 4).

56 Juma (2011).

57 Jarosz (2012: 198).

58 Russell *et al.* (2011).

Chapter 4

1 Frenken (2005: 26).

2   See www.dr-congo.climatemps.com/.
3   See www.brazil.climatemps.com/.
4   Gourou (1970: 279).
5   UNEP (2011a: 10). This 20,000-kilometre estimate by the Food and Agriculture Organization of the United Nations (FAO) is 5,000 kilometres higher than the one published by E.-J. Devroey in what was at the time the most exhaustive study of the Belgian Congo's water assets (Devroey 1951: 8).
6   Michel (2006: 15).
7   Harms (1981).
8   Lederer (1965: 50).
9   Kalron (2010: 111).
10 'Restoring a disappearing giant: Lake Chad', World Bank, 27 March 2014. Available at www.worldbank.org/en/news/feature/2014/03/27/restoring-a-disappearing-giant-lake-chad.
11 See www.cima.ca/cgi-cs/cs.waframe.content?lang=2&click=161647.
12 The connection between the absence of electricity and climate change is made in greater detail in Chapter 2.
13 'Update 2: Congo's copper province governor rejects export ban', Reuters, 18 April 2013. Available at www.reuters.com/article/2013/04/18/congo-democratic-copper-idUSL5N0D53AN20130418.
14 'Country highlights: Congo, Dem. Rep. 2013', World Bank. Available at www.enterprisesurveys.org/data/exploreeconomies/2013/congo-dem-rep.
15 *Ibid.*
16 'Le premier atlas interactif des énergies renouvelables en RDC'. Available at www.cd.undp.org/content/dam/dem_rep_congo/docs/eenv/UNDP-CD-ATLAS-ENERGIE-RENOUVELABLES-RDC.pdf. See also République Démocratique du Congo and Ministère des Ressources Hydrauliques et Électricité (2014).
17 How much energy is 500 kilowatts? The average single family home (in developed industrial societies) consumes between 500 kilowatts and 2,000 kilowatts per year.
18 'The Democratic Republic of the Congo fixes October 2015 as the date for the launch of the first phase of the largest hydroelectric plant in the world', PR Newswire, 18 May 2013. Available at www.prnewswire.com/news-releases/the-democratic-republic-of-the-congo-fixes-october-2015-as-the-date-for-the-launch-of-the-first-phase-of-the-largest-hydroelectric-plant-in-the-world-208008181.html.
19 St-Pierre *et al.* (2013: 15).
20 Misser (2013b).
21 Willame (1986).
22 The $80 billion estimate for Grand Inga includes transmission costs.
23 See www.congress.gov/113/bills/hr3547/BILLS-113hr3547enr.pdf.

24 Misser (2014).
25 'DR Congo Inga Three dam: BHP Billiton withdraws custom', BBC News, 16 February 2012. Available at www.bbc.com/news/world-africa-17056918.
26 'SA, Russia agree to $50-billion nuclear deal', *Mail & Guardian*, 23 September 2014. Available at http://mg.co.za/article/2014-09-23-sa-russia-agree-to-50-billion-nuclear-deal.
27 Willame (1986).
28 Sustainable Energy for All *et al.* (2013).
29 Arnould (2005).
30 'RDC: Justin Kalumba fait un constat malheureux sur la Régie des Voies Fluviales', *Kongo Times!*, 15 June 2012. Available at http://afrique.kongotimes.info/eco_tech/4423-congo-regie-des-voies-fluviales-constat-malheureux.html.
31 Rackley (2006).
32 UNEP (2011a: 27–8).
33 'Millennium Development Goal drinking water target met: sanitation target still lagging far behind', World Health Organization and UNICEF, 6 March 2012. Available at www.who.int/mediacentre/news/releases/2012/drinking_water_20120306/en/.
34 UNEP (2011a: 31).
35 Mouzon (2012: 9).
36 Oxfam (2001: 31).
37 'RDC: une épidémie "touche à sa fin" (MSF)', *Le Figaro*, 29 July 2014. Available at www.lefigaro.fr/flash-actu/2014/07/29/97001-20140729FILWWW00162-rdc-une-epidemie-touche-a-sa-fin-msf.php.
38 Unless stated otherwise, information in this paragraph comes from Mouzon (2012).
39 Tsakala Munikengi and Bongo-Pasi Moke Sangol (2004: 93).
40 Mouzon (2012: 33).
41 Maractho Mudzo Mwacan and Trefon (2004: 40)
42 UNEP (2011a: 24).
43 Lothe and Luamba (2013: 1–3).
44 Harms (1987: 108).
45 Eba'a Atyi and Bayol (2009: 122). Jos Snoeks, a fish expert at the Royal Museum for Central Africa, says that there could be at least 200 fish species not yet identified. Interview, Brussels, November 2014.
46 Mabeka Mantuika (2008: 6).
47 Interview with Professors Mutambwe Shango and Jean-Claude Micha, Kinshasa, September 2014.
48 République du Zaïre (1987: 4).
49 SOFRECO (2012: 9).
50 Interview with Francine Luhusu, Luki, March 2015.
51 Biloko (2015).

52 FAO (2012: 26).

53 'Farmed fish production overtakes beef', Earth Policy Institute, 12 June 2013. Available at www.earth-policy.org/plan_b_updates/2013/update114.

54 Micha (2013: 4).

55 'Pêche et aquaculture: projet de développement de la pêche artisanale et de l'aquaculture au Katanga (PRODEPA AK)', CTB and Ministère de l'Agriculture, Pêche et Élevage, March 2010. Available at www.btcctb.org/files/web/Projet% 20de%20d%C3%A9veloppement%20de%20la%20p%C3%AAche%20 artisanale%20et%20de%20l'aquaculture%20au%20Katanga.pdf.

56 SOFRECO (2012).

57 Micha (2013: 7).

58 Mbalanda Kisoka *et al.* (n.d.: 7).

59 République Démocratique du Congo (2012: 7–8).

60 See www.un.org/waterforlifedecade/iwrm.shtml.

Chapter 5

1 Pilipili Mawezi (2010: 11).

2 Yates (2012: 72).

3 Hodges (2001: 129)

4 Ferguson (2005: 378).

5 Hicks (2015).

6 Interview with Thierry De Putter, January 2014.

7 Trefon (2013: 147–8).

8 'France–Afrique: Le lobby français qui pousse Hollande à Kinshasa', Risques Internationaux, October 2012. Available at www.risques-internationaux.com/ acceslibre/articles%20acces%20libre/LO%20FranceAfriqueoct12.htm.

9 Augé (2012: 11).

10 Pilipili Mawezi (2010: 12).

11 International Crisis Group (2012: 9).

12 Joye and Lewin (1961: 233).

13 Delvaux and Fernandez (2015).

14 Malu (1970: 3–4).

15 Banque Centrale du Congo (2012: 134).

16 L'ordonnance-loi no. 67-231 of 11 May 1967.

17 L'ordonnance-loi no. 81-013 of 2 April 1981.

18 Pilipili Mawezi (2010: 24).

19 Loi no. 007/2002 of 15 July 2002.

20 Leonard (2013); Yates (2012).

21 'Congo parliament adopts new hydrocarbons code', Reuters, 17 June 2015. Available at http://uk.reuters.com/article/2015/06/16/congodemocratic-oil-idUKL5N0Z24ET20150616.

22 Hicks (2015).

23 Misser (2012: 202).

24 Turner (2013: 68).

25 Prunier (2009: 249–55).

26 Misser (2012: 193); International Crisis Group (2006: 4).

27 International Crisis Group (2012: 3).

28 Misser (2013c: 164).

29 UN Panel of Inquiry (2009).

30 'Congo fails to reveal loss-making oil deal with controversial businessman's offshore firm', Global Witness, 23 January 2014. Available at www.global witness.org/en/archive/congo-fails-reveal-loss-making-oil-deal-controversial-businessmans-offshore-firm/.

31 Johnson (2003: 25). For further information on conflict in Ituri, see International Crisis Group (2003).

32 Lujala (2009).

33 Anderson and Browne (2011).

34 See www.heritageoilplc.com/our-operations.aspx.

35 Roberts (2006: 13).

36 Augé (2012: 6).

37 See www.eia.gov/countries/country-data.cfm?fips=ug.

38 Tullow Oil (2013: 13).

39 de Kock (2012: 54).

40 Augé (2012: 12).

41 Global Witness (2012: 29).

42 Augé (2009: 176).

43 'Congo threatens to take back oil blocks', Financial Times, 24 June 2012. Available at www.ft.com/cms/s/0/a5aea554-bc8f-11e1-a470-00144feabdc0.html#axzz3G9OtDBrB.

44 Augé and Nakayi (2013: 5–6).

45 de Kock (2012: 54).

46 Cammaert and Blyth (2013).

47 'Gertler's oil company says Congo project has 3 billion barrels', Bloomberg Business, 7 August 2014. Available at www.bloomberg.com/news/2014-08-07/gertler-s-oil-company-says-congo-project-has-3-billion-barrels.html.

48 Africa Energy Intelligence, no. 643, 1 December 2011.

49 Interview with Amy Shifflette, August 2014.

50 Akpomera (2015).

51 Yates (2012: 72).

52 WWF and Dalberg (2013: 34).

53 d'Huart and Kalpers (2006).

54 African Energy, issue 203, 18 February 2011, p. 15.

55 'Vote en Commission d'une résolution de Georges Dallemagne pour assurer

la protection du Parc des Virunga', Belgian Federal Parliament, 20 November 2012. Available at www.cdh-parlementfederal.be/?p=4054p://.

56 'Africa Great Lakes peace initiative', Howard G. Buffett Foundation. Available at www.thehowardgbuffettfoundation.org/initiatives/africa-great-lakes-peace-initiative/.

57 *African Energy*, issue 203, 18 February 2011, p. 16; Kihangani Bindu (2011: 11).

58 Global Witness (2014: 12–13).

59 WWF and Dalberg (2013: 28).

60 Public Order Act of 1969 on the conservation of nature and the 2002 Mining Code.

61 See www.un.org/en/decolonization/declaration.shtml.

62 'UNESCO sacrifices wildlife preserve for uranium mine', Rainforest Rescue. Available at www.rainforest-rescue.org/mailalert/883/unesco-sacrifices-wildlife-preserve-for-uranium-mine.

63 He is controversial because, under his watch, there have been increased problems with local populations who accuse him of acting like the 'president of the National Republic of Virunga'. 'Howard Buffett bets on hydropower to rebuild eastern Congo', Reuters, 20 August 2015. Available at www.reuters.com/article/2015/08/20/us-congodemocratic-buffett-idUSKCN0QP13V20150820.

64 See http://virungamovie.com/.

65 'Bill Clinton makes surprise appearance at Leonardo DiCaprio's "Virunga" screening', *Hollywood Reporter*, 31 January 2015. Available at www.hollywood reporter.com/news/bill-cliton-surprises-leonardo-dicaprio-768852.

66 'Le directeur belge du parc des Virunga hors de danger', LaLibre.be, 15 April 2014. Available at www.lalibre.be/actu/international/le-directeur-belge-du-parc-des-virunga-hors-de-danger-534d832b3570aae038b8249f.

67 'Soco denies paying for Congo DRC trip to UN to discuss Virunga oil drilling', *Guardian*, 19 June 2014. Available at www.theguardian.com/environment/2014/jun/19/soco-congo-drc-virunga-oil-unesco-doha.

68 Augé and Nakayi (2013: 4).

69 Interview with François Misser, July 2014.

70 Taylor (2014: 351).

Chapter 6

1 'How Dodd–Frank is failing Congo', Foreign Policy, 2 February 2015. Available at https://foreignpolicy.com/2015/02/02/how-dodd-frank-is-failing-congo-mining-conflict-minerals/.

2 World Bank (2008: 13).

3 This table seems to reveal some inconsistencies and is presented merely as an indicator. Other sources place Botswana or Canada as the world's leader in diamond reserves, for example.

4   See the 'Summary of the environmental and social impact assessment (ESIA)'
     at www.afdb.org/fileadmin/uploads/afdb/Documents/Environmental-and-
     Social-Assessments/DRC%20-%20Nyumba%20Ya%20Akiba%20Cement%
     20Plant%20-%20ESIA%20Summary.pdf.

5   Congo has almost no gem-quality diamonds.

6   Mantz (2008: 37).

7   Coltan is an abbreviation for the columbite–tantalite ore minerals. It is a source
     of niobium and tantalum metals. It is the tantalum that is used in capacitors
     (devices that store energy).

8   Nest (2011).

9   See http://tanb.org/coltan.

10   National Research Council (2008: 48).

11   Banza et al. (2009).

12   'Exclusive: Congo under scrutiny over Hezbollah business links', Reuters,
     16 March 2012. Available at www.reuters.com/article/2012/03/16/us-congo-
     democratic-hezbollah-idUSBRE82F0TT20120316.

13   Herzog (2013: 153–7). See also 'Sting unravels stunning mafia plot', Nuclear
     Threat Initiative (NTI), 12 January 1999. Available at www.nti.org/analysis/
     articles/sting-unravels-stunning-mafia-plot/.

14   de Maret (1985).

15   Stengers (1982).

16   Renton et al. (2007).

17   Mupepele (2012: 122).

18   Rubbers (2013).

19   Slade (1961: 2–4).

20   Domergue and Mpoyi Mbunga (2012: 108).

21   Bezy et al. (1981: 164–5).

22   Rubbers (2013: 45).

23   Petit and Mulumbwa Mutambwa (2005: 470).

24   Gérard-Libois (1966).

25   Larmer and Kennes (2014).

26   Ndikumana and Boyce (1998).

27   For an interesting overview of some of the terms used to describe these
     strategies, see Trapido (2015: 20–2).

28   Kennes (2005: 167).

29   Leclercq (2001: 52–3).

30   Kennes (2002: 605).

31   Mazalto (2009).

32   Vlassenroot and Raeymaekers (2008).

33   This was revealed in the report of the Lutundula Commission (République
     Démocratique du Congo and Assemblée Nationale 2005: 97).

34   Although the company is registered in Belgium, the family was originally from
     New Zealand. See www.forrestgroup.com/en/gfi.html.

35 Kennes (1999).
36 Some of the companies involved were American Mineral Fields, Banro Resource Corporation, Barrick Gold Corporation, Trillion Resources, Diamond Works, First Quantum Minerals, International Panorama Resource Corp., Melkior Resources Inc. and Samax Gold Inc.
37 'First Quantum gets out of Congo with $1.25 billion asset sale', Mining.com, 5 January 2012. Available at www.mining.com/first-quantum-gets-out-of-congo-with-1-25-billion-asset-sale/.
38 World Bank (2010).
39 *Ibid.*: 58.
40 De Putter and Decrée (2013: 54).
41 *Ibid.*: 56.
42 World Vision (2013).
43 André and Godin (2014).
44 Geenen (2012: 327).
45 Jackson (2002: 528); Jacquemot (2009: 43).
46 Lubamba (2006).
47 Bulzomi *et al.* (2014).
48 de Failly (2001).
49 For a good description of the multiple levels of middlemen in the artisanal diamond sector, see Blore (2012).
50 Cuvelier (2011), notably Chapter 1.
51 Vlassenroot and Raeymaekers (2008: 50).
52 Geenen (2012: 327).
53 *Ibid.*
54 De Boeck (2001: 557).
55 Cuvelier (2011), notably Chapter 3.
56 Mantz (2008: 43).
57 Smith (2011: 22).
58 UN Panel of Inquiry (2009).
59 A number of scholars have analysed the conflict mineral debate, including Autesserre (2012), Cuvelier (2010), Cuvelier *et al.* (2014), De Putter and Delvaux (2013), Johnson (2013) and Turner (2013).
60 See www.enoughproject.org/.
61 See www.easterncongo.org/.
62 The Kimberley Process assists governments, industry and civil society in stemming the flow of rough diamonds used by rebel movements to finance wars against legitimate governments (see www.kimberleyprocess.com/).
63 For an overview of the different international initiatives set up to tackle the traceability of Congo's minerals, see Johnson (2013: 9–15) and De Putter and Delvaux (2013: 104).
64 Cuvelier *et al.* (2014: 2).

65 Mantz, personal communication, January 2015.

66 Johnson (2013: 7).

67 Cuvelier *et al.* (2014: 31).

68 See www.parl.gc.ca/HousePublications/Publication.aspx?Language=E&Mode =1&DocId=6062040&File=4&Col=1.

69 Prunier (2009: 235–8).

70 de Villers (2009: 227).

71 World Bank (1992: xiii–xiv).

72 Mazalto (2009: 176).

73 The 'Direction générale de recettes administratives, domaniales et judiciaires', the 'Direction générale des impôts' and the 'Direction générale des douanes et accises'.

74 World Bank (2010: 13).

75 Rubbers (2010: 329).

76 Rubbers (2013: 56).

77 République Démocratique du Congo and Ministère des Infrastructures, Travaux Publics et Reconstruction (2007).

78 Marysse and Geenen (2009).

79 Global Witness (2011).

80 'MP alleges $5.5bn loss from Congolese mining deals', OneWorld News, 22 November 2011. Available at www.oneworld.org/2011/11/22/mp-alleges-55bn-loss-from-congolese-mining-deals.

81 *Ibid.*

82 Africa Progress Panel (2013: 56).

83 *Ibid.*: 56–7.

84 See https://eiti.org/eiti.

85 For more on Publish What You Pay, see www.resourcegovernance.org/ training/resource_center/backgrounders/publish-what-you-pay-pwyp.

86 For more on PROMINES, see www.prominesrdc.cd/.

87 Trefon (2011a: 113–15).

88 UNEP (2011b: 32).

89 Cheyns *et al.* (2014).

90 Zaragosa Montejano (2013).

91 Global Witness (2011: 35).

92 EITI (2012: 25).

93 Jackson (2014: 5).

94 ITIE (2014: 38–40, 92–5).

95 Marysse and Tshimanga (2013: 27).

96 'Freeport to buy Phelps Dodge for $26B', *Forbes*, 20 November 2006. Available at www.forbes.com/2006/11/20/freeport-phelpss-update-markets-equity-cx_po_1120markets10.html.

97 See the obituary of Marc Rich in *The Economist*, 6 July 2013. Available at www.

economist.com/news/obituary/21580438-marc-rich-king-commodities-died-june-26th-aged-78-marc-rich.

98 See www.globalwitness.org/en/campaigns/oil-gas-and-mining/congo-secret-sales/.

99 See www.katangamining.com/operations/key-assets/kamota-underground.aspx.

100 'Katanga Mining announces 2014 year end operational highlights', Katanga Mining news release, 10 February 2015. Available at www.katangamining.com/media/news-releases/2015/2015-02-10.aspx.

101 'Update 1: Glencore Congo unit says to pursue $880 mln modernisation plan', Reuters Africa, 11 September 2015. Available at http://af.reuters.com/article/drcNews/idAFL5N11H3S420150911.

102 'Banro tumbles as Congo gold mine projections fall: Canada credit', Bloomberg, 11 July 2014. Available at www.bloomberg.com/news/2014-07-11/banro-tumbles-as-congo-gold-mine-projections-fall-canada-credit.html.

103 Chambre des Mines (2014: 19).

104 'Samples show that US Rare Earths has potential for high-value europium rich critical rare earths', InvestorIntel, 6 January 2015. Available at http://investorintel.com/technology-metals-intel/samples-show-us-rare-earths-potential-high-value-europim-enriched-rees/.

105 See www.ivanhoemines.com/projects/kamoa-project.

106 'On an African dog and pony show with mining mogul Robert Friedland', CEO. ca, 17 February 2014. Available at http://ceo.ca/2014/02/17/on-an-african-dog-and-pony-show-with-billionaire-mining-mogul-robert-friedland/.

107 Isaacson (2011: 37–40).

108 'Update 1: Congo says Ivanhoe Mines' Kamoa deal should be suspended', Reuters Africa, 16 June 2015. Available at http://af.reuters.com/article/drcNews/idAFL5N0Z24KV20150616.

109 'Update 1: Congo copper production to hold steady in 2015 – mines ministry', Reuters, 15 October 2015. Available at http://uk.reuters.com/article/2015/10/15/congodemocratic-mining-copper-idUKL8N12F2PK20151015.

110 World Bank (2010: 32)

111 *Ibid.*: 1.

112 The German Federal Institute for Geosciences and Natural Resources is involved in supporting the Congolese government to formalise artisanal mining (see www.bgr.bund.de/EN/Themen/Min_rohstoffe/CTC/Mineral-Certification-DRC/Implementation/implementation_drc_node_en.html).

113 See Garrett and Lintzer (2010) for a similar argument.

BIBLIOGRAPHY

Achu Samndong, R. and I. Nhantumbo (2015) *Natural Resources Governance in the Democratic Republic of Congo: Breaking sector walls for sustainable land use investments*. London: International Institute for Environment and Development (IIED).

Africa Progress Panel (2013) *Equity in Extractives. Stewarding Africa's natural resources for all. Africa progress report 2013*. Geneva: Africa Progress Panel.

Akpomera, E. (2015) 'International crude oil theft: elite predatory tendencies in Nigeria', *Review of African Political Economy* 42(143): 156–65.

Anderson, D. M. and A. J. Browne (2011) 'The politics of oil in eastern Africa', *Journal of Eastern African Studies* 5(2): 369–410.

André, G. and M. Godin (2014) 'Child labour, agency and family dynamics: the case of mining in Katanga (DRC)', *Childhood* 21(2): 161–74.

Anseeuw, W. (2013) 'The rush for land in Africa: resource grabbing or green revolution?', *Southern African Journal of International Affairs* 20(1): 159–77.

Arnould, R. (2005) 'La canalisation du fleuve Congo à l'aval de Kinshasa: un défi pour le XXIe siècle', *Bulletin de la Société Géographique de Liège* 46: 99–117.

Augé, B. (2009) 'Border conflicts tied to hydrocarbons in the Great Lakes region of Africa' in J. Lesourne (ed.) *Governance of Oil in Africa: Unfinished business*. Paris: French Institute for International Relations.

— (2012) *L'Afrique de l'Est, une géopolitique pétrolière à haut risque*. Paris: French Institute for International Relations.

Augé, B. and R. Nakayi (2013) *Eastern Africa: A new oil and gas frontier*. Nairobi: Observatoire des Grands Lacs en Afrique.

Autesserre, S. (2012) 'Dangerous tales: dominant narratives on the Congo and their unintended consequences', *African Affairs* 111(443): 202–22.

Banchirigah, S. M. and G. Hilson (2010) 'De-agrarianization, re-agrarianization and local economic development: re-orientating livelihoods in African artisanal mining communities', *Policy Sciences* 43(2): 157–80.

Banque Centrale du Congo (2012) *Rapport annuel 2012*. Kinshasa: Banque Centrale du Congo.

Banza, C., T. S. Nawrot, V. Haufroid, S. Decrée, T. De Putter, E. Smolders, B. Ilunga, O. Numbi, A. Ndala, A. Mwanza and B. Nemery (2009) 'High human exposure to cobalt and other metals in Katanga, a mining area of the Democratic Republic of Congo', *Environmental Research* 109(6): 745–52.

Bayol, N., B. Demarquez, C. de Weissege, R. Eba'a Atyi, J.-F. Fisher, R. Nasi, A. Pasquier, X. Rossi, M. Steil and C. Vivien (2012) 'Forest management and the timber sector in central Africa' in C. de Wasseige, P. de Marcken, N. Bayol, F. Hiol Hiol, P. Mayaux, B. Desclée, R. Nasi, A. Billand, P. Defourny and R. Eba'a Atyi (eds) *The Forests of the Congo Basin: State of the forest 2010*. Luxembourg: European Union.

Bezy, F., J.-P. Peemans and J.-M. Wautelet (1981) *Accumulation et sous-développement au Zaïre 1960–1980*. Louvain-la-Neuve: Presses Universitaires de Louvain.

Billand, A. (2012) 'Biodiversity in central African forests: an overview of knowledge, main challenges and conservation measures' in C. de Wasseige, P. de Marcken, N. Bayol, F. Hiol Hiol, P. Mayaux, B. Desclée, R. Nasi, A. Billand, P. Defourny and R. Eba'a Atyi (eds) *The Forests of the Congo Basin: State of the forest 2010*. Luxembourg: European Union.

Biloko, M. (2015) 'Croissance démographique et demande en bois énergie dans les pêcheries du lac Edouard/PNVi: cas de Vitshumbi et Kyavinyonge'. Unpublished master's thesis, École Régionale Post-universitaire d'Aménagement et de Gestion Intégrés des Forêts et Territoires Tropicaux, University of Kinshasa.

Bisiaux, F., R. Peltier and J.-C. Muliele (2009) 'Plantations industrielles et agroforesterie au service des populations des plateaux Batéké, Mampu, en République démocratique du Congo', *Bois et Forêts des Tropiques* 301(3): 21–32.

Bisschop, L. (2012) 'Out of the woods: the illegal trade in tropical timber and a European trade hub', *Global Crime* 13(3): 191–212.

Blore, S. (2012) 'Trading tenure for formalisation: a new approach to the licensing of artisanal diamond mining in the DRC' in S. Van Bockstael and K. Vlassenroot (eds) *A Farmer's Best Friend? Artisanal diamond mining and rural change in West and Central Africa*. Gent: Academia Press.

Bräutigam, D. and Haisen Zhang (2013) 'Green dreams: myth and reality in China's agricultural investment in Africa', *Third World Quarterly* 34(9): 1676–96.

Brown, M. I. (2013) *Redeeming REDD: Policies, incentives and social feasibility for avoided deforestation*. London and New York: Routledge.

Bryceson, D. (2006) 'Fragile cities: fundamentals of urban life in East and Southern Africa' in D. Bryceson and D. Potts (eds) *African Urban Economies: Viability, vitality or vitiation?* New York: Palgrave Macmillan.

Buelens, F. and S. Marysse (2009) 'Returns on investments during the colonial era: the case of the Belgian Congo', *Economic History Review* 62(S1): 135–66.

Bulzomi, A., F. Hilgert, K. Matthysen, S. Spittaels and Y. Weyns (2014) *Analysis of the Interactive Map of Artisanal Mining Areas in Eastern DR Congo: May 2014 update*. Antwerp: International Peace Information Service.

Cammaert, P. and F. Blyth (2013) 'The UN Intervention Brigade in the Democratic Republic of the Congo'. Issue brief. New York: International Peace Institute.

Chambre des Mines (2014) *Rapport d'activités troisième trimestre 2014*. Kinshasa: Chambre des Mines and Fédération des Entreprises du Congo.

Chausse, J.-P., T. Kembola and R. Ngonde (2012) 'L'agriculture: pierre angulaire de l'économie de la RDC' in J. Herderschee, D. Mukoko Samba and M. Tshimenga Tshibangu (eds) *Résilience d'un géant Africain: Accélérer la croissance et promouvoir l'emploi en République démocratique du Congo*, volume II. Kinshasa: Banque Mondiale and Médiaspaul.

Cheru, F. and R. Modi (2013) 'Introduction: peasants, the state and foreign direct investment in African agriculture' in F. Cheru and R. Modi (eds) *Agricultural Development and Food Security in Africa: The impact of Chinese, Indian and Brazilian investments*. Uppsala and London: Nordic Africa Institute and Zed Books.

Chevallier, R. and M.-L. du Preez (2012) *Timber Trade in Africa's Great Lakes: The road from Beni, DRC to Kampala, Uganda*. Johannesburg: South African Institute for International Affairs.

Cheyns, K., C. Banza, L. Kabamba, J. Ngoy, V. Haufroid, T. De Putter, T. Nawrot, C. Muleka, O. Luboya, B. Kabyla, B. Nemery and E. Smolders (2014) 'Pathways of human exposure to cobalt in Katanga, a mining area of the D.R. Congo', *Science of the Total Environment* 490: 313–21.

Clark, J. F. (ed.) (2002) *The African Stakes of the Congo War*. New York and Kampala: Palgrave and Fountain.

Cleaver, F. (2012) *Development Through Bricolage: Rethinking institutions for natural resource management*. London: Routledge.

Cleaver, K. M. and G. A. Schreiber (1994) *Reversing the Spiral: The population, agriculture, and environment nexus in sub-Saharan Africa*. Washington, DC: World Bank.

Colom Bickford, A. (2016) 'Conversion to conservation: beliefs and practices of the conservation community in the Congo Basin (1960–present)'. Unpublished doctoral thesis, Catholic University of Leuven (KUL).

Commission on Climate and Tropical Forests (2009) *Protecting the Climate Forests: Why reducing tropical deforestation is in America's vital national interest*. Washington, DC: Commission on Climate and Tropical Forests.

Cotula, L. (2013) *The Great African Land Grab? Agricultural investments and the global food system*. London: Zed Books.

Counsell, S. (2006) *Forest Governance in the Democratic Republic of Congo: An NGO perspective*. Moreton-in-Marsh and Brussels: FERN.

Credit Suisse, World Wildlife Fund and McKinsey & Company (2014) *Conservation Finance: Moving beyond donor-driven funding toward an investor-driven approach*. Zurich: Credit Suisse, World Wildlife Fund and McKinsey & Company.

Cuvelier, J. (ed.) (2010) *The Complexity of Resource Governance in a Context of State Fragility: The case of Eastern DRC*. London and Antwerp: International Alert and International Peace Information Service (IPIS).

— (2011) 'Men, mines and masculinities: the lives and practices of artisanal miners in Lwambo (Katanga province, DR Congo)'. Unpublished doctoral thesis, Catholic University of Leuven (KUL).

Cuvelier, J., S. Van Bockstael, K. Vlassenroot and C. Iguma (2014) *Analyzing the Impact of the Dodd-Frank Act on Congolese Livelihoods*. New York: Social Science Research Council.

d'Huart, J.-P. and J. Kalpers (2006) 'Le besoin d'une restructuration institutionnelle de l'ICCN au sortir de la période de conflit' in M. Languy and E. de Merode (eds) *Virunga: Survie du premier parc d'Afrique*. Tielt (Belgium): Lannoo.

De Boeck, F. (2001) '*Garimeiro* worlds: digging, dying and "hunting" for diamonds in Angola', *Review of African Political Economy* 28(90): 548–62.

de Failly, D. (2001) 'Coltan: pour comprendre …' in S. Marysse and F. Reyntjens (eds) *L'Afrique des Grands Lacs: Annuaire 2000–2001*. Paris: L'Harmattan.

de Kock, P. (2012) 'Fuelling or dousing regional fires? Uganda's rising power in Africa' in P. de Kock and K. Sturman, *The Power of Oil: Charting Uganda's transition to a petro-state*. Johannesburg: South African Institute for International Affairs.

de Maret, P. (1985) 'Recent archaeological research and dates from Central Africa', *Journal of African History* 26(2/3): 129–48.

De Putter, T. and S. Decrée (2013) 'Le potentiel minier de la République Démocratique du Congo (RDC): mythes et composantes d'une "dynamique minière"' in S. Marysse and J. Omasombo Tshonda (eds) *Conjoncture congolaise 2012: Politique, secteur minier et gestion des ressources naturelles en RD Congo*. Tervuren and Paris: Royal Museum for Central Africa and L'Harmattan.

De Putter, T. and C. Delvaux (2013) 'Certifier les ressources minérales dans la région des Grands Lacs', *Politique Etrangère* 78(2): 99–112.

de Villers, G. (2009) *République démocratique du Congo. De la guerre aux élections: L'ascension de Joseph Kabila et la Troisième République (janvier 2001–août 2008)*. Tervuren and Paris: Institut africain-CEDAF and L'Harmattan.

de Wasseige C., D. Devers, P. de Marcken, R. Eba'a Atyi, R. Nasi and P. Mayaux (eds) (2009) *The Forests of the Congo Basin: State of the forest 2008*. Luxembourg: European Union.

Debroux, L., T. Hart, D. Kaimowitz, A. Karsenty and G. Topa (eds) (2007) *Forests in Post-conflict Democratic Republic of Congo: Analysis of a priority agenda*. Bogor (Indonesia), Washington, DC and Montpellier: Center for International Forestry Research (CIFOR), World Bank and Centre de Coopération Internationale en Recherche Agronomique pour le Développement (CIRAD).

Delegation of the European Commission (2006) 'Revue institutionnelle et programme de renforcement de l'ICCN et de l'IJZBC'. Unpublished report. Brussels: AGRECO.

Delvaux, D. and M. Fernandez (2015) 'Petroleum potential of the Congo Basin' in M. de Wit, F. Guillochau and M. C. J. de Wit (eds) *The Geology and Resource Potential of the Congo Basin*. Berlin: Springer.

Demunter, P. (1975) *Masses rurales et luttes politiques au Zaïre: Le processus de politisation des masses rurales au Bas-Zaïre.* Paris: Éditions Anthropos.

Devroey, E.-J. (1951) *Observations hydrographiques au Congo Belge et au Ruanda-Urundi (1948–1950).* Brussels: Institut Royal Colonial Belge.

Domergue, C. and A. Mpoyi Mbunga (2012) 'La gestion des ressources naturelles pour une croissance durable' in J. Herderschee, D. Mukoko Samba and M. Tshimenga Tshibangu (eds) *Résilience d'un géant Africain: Accélérer la croissance et promouvoir l'emploi en République Démocratique du Congo. Vol. II: études sectorielles.* Kinshasa: Médiaspaul.

Doumenge, C. (1990) *La conservation des écosystèmes forestiers du Zaïre.* Gland (Switzerland): International Union for the Conservation of Nature.

Duffield, M. (2014) 'From immersion to simulation: remote methodologies and the decline of area studies', *Review of African Political Economy* 41(143): S75 S95.

Eba'a Atyi, R. and N. Bayol with S. Malele Mbala, J. Tunguni, P. Mwamba Kyungu and F. Yata (2009) 'The forests of the Democratic Republic of Congo in 2008' in C. de Wasseige, D. Devers, P. de Marcken, R. Eba'a Atyi, R. Nasi and P. Mayaux (eds) *The Forests of the Congo Basin: State of the forest 2008.* Luxembourg: European Union.

EITI (2012) *Report: Democratic Republic of the Congo, 2010.* Kinshasa: Extractive Industries Transparency Initiative (EITI).

— (2014) *Report: Democratic Republic of the Congo, 2012.* Kinshasa: Extractive Industries Transparency Initiative (EITI).

Englebert, P. (2014) *Democratic Republic of Congo: Growth for all? Challenges and opportunities for a new economic future.* Johannesburg: The Brenthurst Foundation.

Ernst, C., P. Mayaux, A. Verhegghen, C. Bodart, M. Christophe and P. Defourny (2013) 'National forest cover change in Congo Basin: deforestation, reforestation, degradation and regeneration for the years 1990, 2000 and 2005', *Global Change Biology* 19(4): 1173–87.

Ernst, C., A. Verhegghen, P. Mayaux, M. Hansen and P. Defourny (2012) 'Central African forest cover and cover change mapping' in C. de Wasseige, P. de Marcken, N. Bayol, F. Hiol Hiol, P. Mayaux, B. Desclée, R. Nasi, A. Billand, P. Defourny and R. Eba'a Atyi (eds) *The Forests of the Congo Basin: State of the forest 2010.* Luxembourg: European Union.

Fairhead, J. and M. Leach (1998) *Reframing Deforestation. Global analyses and local realities: Studies in West Africa.* London and New York: Routledge.

FAO (2012) *The State of World Fisheries and Aquaculture 2012.* Rome: Food and Agriculture Organization of the United Nations (FAO).

Ferguson, J. (2005) 'Seeing like an oil company: space, security, and global capital in neoliberal Africa', *American Anthropologist* 107(3): 377–82.

FERN and Forest Peoples Programme (2014) 'Implement in haste, repent at leisure: a call for rethinking the World Bank's carbon fund, based on an analysis of the DRC ER-PIN'. Briefing paper. Moreton-in-Marsh and Brussels: FERN and Forest Peoples Programme.

Frenken, K. (ed.) (2005) *Irrigation in Africa in Figures: AQUASTAT survey 2005*. Rome: Food and Agriculture Organization of the United Nations (FAO).

Garrett, N. and M. Lintzer (2010) 'Can Katanga's mining sector drive growth and development in the DRC?', *Journal of Eastern African Studies* 4(3): 400–24.

Geenen, S. (2012) 'A dangerous bet: the challenges of formalizing artisanal mining in the Democratic Republic of Congo', *Resources Policy* 37(3): 322–30.

Geist, H. J. and E. F. Lambin (2002) 'Proximate causes and underlying driving forces of tropical deforestation', *BioScience* 52(2): 143–50.

Gérard-Libois, J. (1966) *Katanga Secession*. Madison: University of Wisconsin Press.

Global Witness (2011) *Congo and China: Friends in need*. London: Global Witness.

— (2012) *Rigged? The scramble for Africa's oil, gas and minerals*. London: Global Witness.

— (2014) *Drillers in the Mist: How secret payments and a climate of violence helped UK firm open African national park to oil*. London: Global Witness.

Gourou, P. (1970) *L'Afrique*. Paris: Hachette.

GRAIN (2013) 'Land grabbing for biofuels must stop: EU biofuel policies are displacing communities and starving the planet'. Barcelona: GRAIN.

GRAIN and RIAO-RDC (2015) 'Agro-colonialisme au Congo: les institutions financières de développement européennes et américaines financent une nouvelle phase d'agro-colonialisme au Congo'. Barcelona: GRAIN.

Greenpeace (2012) '"Exploitation artisanale" = exploitation industrielle forestière déguisée'. Kinshasa: Greenpeace.

Hanson, K. T., F. Owusu and C. D'Alessandro (2014) 'Toward a coordinated approach to natural resource management in Africa' in K. T. Hanson, C. D'Alessandro and F. Owusu (eds) *Managing Africa's Natural Resources: Capacities for development*. London and New York: Palgrave.

Harms, R. (1981) *River of Wealth, River of Sorrow: The central Zaire basin in the era of the slave and ivory trade, 1500–1981*. New Haven: Yale University Press.

— (1987) *Games Against Nature: An eco-cultural history of the Nunu of equatorial Africa*. Cambridge: Cambridge University Press.

Herderschee, J., K.-A. Kaiser and D. Mukoko Samba (2012) *Resilience of an African Giant: Boosting growth and development in the Democratic Republic of Congo*. Washington, DC: World Bank.

Herzog, R. (2013) *A Short History of Nuclear Folly: Mad scientists, dithering Nazis, lost nukes, and catastrophic cover-ups*. New York: Melville House.

Heyse, T. (1940) 'La politique des concessions foncières au Congo belge', *Revue d'Histoire Moderne* 15(41/42): 88–104.

Hicks, C. (2015) *Africa's New Oil: Power, pipelines and future fortunes*. London: Zed Books.

Hoare, A. (2007) *Clouds on the Horizon: The Congo Basin's forests and climate change.* London: The Rainforest Foundation.

Hochschild, A. (1998) *King Leopold's Ghost: A story of greed, terror and heroism in colonial Africa.* Boston and New York: Houghton Mifflin Company.

Hodges, T. (2001) *Angola: From Afro-Stalinism to petro-diamond capitalism.* Oxford and Bloomington: James Currey and Indiana University Press.

Huart, A. and C. Tombu (2010) *Congo: Les 4 trésors.* Neufchâteau (Belgium): Weyrich Edition.

Huart, A., C. Vangu, M. Rodriguez, B. Hugel, B. Perrodeau, R. C. Pembe, P. Ossit, P. Ngolo, A. Nkoba, T. Kalulu, J. Aloni, E. Bisimwa, P. Mivimba and S. Malembe (2013) 'Une relance économique durable en RDC base sur le développement rural décentralisé, la professionnalisation de l'agriculture, en préservant les ressources naturelles en RDC: note stratégique'. Unpublished report, Kinshasa.

International Crisis Group (2003) *Congo Crisis: Military intervention in Ituri.* Nairobi, New York and Brussels: International Crisis Group.

— (2006) *Securing Congo's Elections: Lessons from the Kinshasa showdown.* Nairobi and Brussels: International Crisis Group.

— (2012) *Black Gold in the Congo: Threat to stability or development opportunity?* Kinshasa, Nairobi and Brussels: International Crisis Group.

Isaacson, W. (2011) *Steve Jobs.* London: Little, Brown.

ITIE (2014) *Rapport de conciliation ITIE, RDC, exercice 2012.* Kinshasa: Initiative pour la Transparence dans les Industries Extractives (ITIE).

Jackson, S. (2002) 'Making a killing: criminality and coping in the Kivu war economy', *Review of African Political Economy* 29(93/94): 517–36.

Jackson, T. (2014) *Survey of Mining Companies 2014.* Vancouver: Fraser Institute.

Jacquemot, P. (2009) 'Ressources minérales, armes et violences dans les Kivus (RDC)', *Hérodote* 134: 38–62.

Jansson, C., A. Westerbergh, J. Zhang, X. Hud and C. Sun (2009) 'Cassava, a potential biofuel crop in (the) People's Republic of China', *Applied Energy* 86(S1): S95–S99.

Jarosz, L. (2012) 'Growing inequality: agricultural revolutions and the political ecology of rural development', *International Journal of Agricultural Sustainability* 10(2): 192–9.

Javelle, A.-G. and P. Veit (2012) *Managing Land for Mining and Conservation in the Democratic Republic of Congo.* Washington, DC: Africa Biodiversity Collaborative Group. Available at www.wri.org/blog/2012/08/managing-land-mining-and-conservation-democratic-republic-congo.

Jewsiewicki, B. (1979) 'Zaire enters the world system: its colonial incorporation as the Belgian Congo, 1885–1960' in G. Gran (ed.) *Zaire: The political economy of underdevelopment.* New York: Praeger.

Johnson, D. (2003) *Shifting Sands: Oil exploration in the Rift Valley and the Congo conflict*. Goma: Pole Institute.

— (2013) *No Kivu, No Conflict? The misguided struggle against 'conflict minerals' in the DRC*. Goma: Pole Institute.

Joye, P. and R. Lewin (1961) *Les Trusts du Congo*. Brussels: Société Populaire d'Éditions.

Juma, C. (2011) *The New Harvest: Agricultural innovation in Africa*. Oxford: Oxford University Press.

Kalron, N. (2010) 'A "transparent gold" rush', *African Security Review* 19(3): 110–13.

Karsenty, A. (2010) *Large-scale Acquisition of Rights on Forest Lands in Africa*. Washington, DC: Rights and Resources Initiative.

— (2012) 'Forêts: les promesses non tenues des instruments économiques', *Economie Appliquée* 65(2): 137–67.

Kearsley, E., T. de Haulleville, K. Hufkens, A. Kidimbu, B. Toirambe, G. Baert, D. Huygens, Y. Kebede, P. Defourny, J. Bogaert, H. Beeckman, K. Steppe, P. Boeckx and H. Verbeeck (2013) 'Conventional tree height–diameter relationships significantly overestimate aboveground carbon stocks in the Central Congo Basin', *Nature Communications*, vol. 4, article no. 2269.

Kennes, E. (1999) 'Le secteur minier au Congo: "déconnexion" et descente aux enfers' in S. Marysse and F. Reyntjens (eds) *L'Afrique des Grands Lacs: Annuaire 1998–1999*. Paris: L'Harmattan.

— (2002) 'Footnotes to the mining sector', *Review of African Political Economy* 29(93/94): 601–7.

— (2005) 'The Democratic Republic of the Congo: structures of greed, networks of need' in C. J. Arnson and I. W. Zartman (eds) *Rethinking the Economies of War: The intersection of need, creed, and greed*. Washington, DC and Baltimore: Woodrow Wilson Center Press and Johns Hopkins University Press.

Kihangi Bindu, K. (2011) *L'exploitation du pétrole du lac Edouard et la loi environnementale en République Démocratique du Congo*. Johannesburg: Centre for International Sustainable Development Law.

Kipalu, P. and J. Mukungu (2013) *The Status of the REDD+ Process in the Democratic Republic of Congo*. Kinshasa: Forest Peoples Programme.

Larmer, M. and E. Kennes (2014) 'Rethinking the Katangese secession', *Journal of Imperial and Commonwealth History* 42(4): 741–61.

Le Plae, E. (1939) 'Native agricultural policy and European agriculture in the Belgian Congo', *African Affairs* 38(152): 357–69.

Le Roy, E. (1991) 'Introduction générale' in E. Le Bris, E. Le Roy and P. Mathieu (eds) *L'appropriation de la terre en Afrique noire: Manuel d'analyses, de décision et de gestion*. Paris: Karthala.

Leclercq, H. (2001) 'Le rôle économique du diamant dans le conflit congolais' in L. Monnier, B. Jewsiewicki and G. de Villers (eds) *Chasse au diamant au Congo/Zaïre*. Tervuren and Paris: Royal Museum for Central Africa and L'Harmattan.

Lederer, A. (1965) *Histoire de la navigation au Congo.* Tervuren: Royal Museum for Central Africa.

Leitenberg, M. (1981) 'Satellite launchers – and potential ballistic missiles – on the commercial market', *Current Research on Peace and Violence* 4(2): 114–28.

Leonard, R. (2013) 'A new oil world: the game has changed, but how? Africa is becoming a major new player in the new world hydrocarbon order', *American Foreign Policy Interests* 35(6): 352–9.

Lescuyer, G., P. O. Cerutti, E. E. Mendoula, R. Eba'a Atyi and R. Nasi (2012) 'An appraisal of chainsaw milling in the Congo Basin' in C. de Wasseige, P. de Marcken, N. Bayol, F. Hiol Hiol, P. Mayaux, B. Desclée, R. Nasi, A. Billand, P. Defourny and R. Eba'a Atyi (eds) *The Forests of the Congo Basin: State of the forest 2010.* Luxembourg: European Union.

Lothe, P. and J.-J. Luamba (2013) 'Programme pilote de réhabilitation et de développement des systèmes d'appropriation en eau potable et d'assainissement en RD Congo (RDC0504312 et RDC0708811): projets AEPA Sud Kivu, Maniema/Kindu, Kinshasa-Est et Lemba & Patu. Mission d'évaluation finale'. Louvain-La-Neuve: Hydro-R&D International.

Lubamba, J.-B. (2006) 'Les conditions de vie et de travail des creuseurs artisanaux de diamant de la ville de Mbuji Mayi'. Unpublished report. Kinshasa: Réseau Ressources Naturelles.

Lujala, P. (2009) 'Deadly combat over natural resources: gems, petroleum, drugs, and the severity of armed conflict', *Journal of Conflict Resolution* 53(1): 50–71.

Mabeka Mantuika, J. (2008) 'Etude diagnostique des pêches maritimes en République Démocratique du Congo'. Unpublished report. Kinshasa: Food and Agriculture Organization of the United Nations (FAO).

Maldague, M., S. Mankoto and T. Rakotomavo (1997) *Notions d'aménagement et de développement intégrés des forêts tropicales.* Paris: UNESCO.

Malu, F. (1970) 'Le système énergétique de la République Démocratique de Congo'. Kinshasa: Office National de la Recherche et du Développement.

Mantz, J. W. (2008) 'Improvisational economies: coltan production in the eastern Congo', *Social Anthropology* 19(1): 34–50.

Maractho Mudzo Mwacan, A. and T. Trefon (2004) 'The tap is on strike: water (non)distribution and supply strategies' in T. Trefon (ed.) *Reinventing Order in the Congo: How people respond to state failure in Kinshasa.* London: Zed Books.

Marien, J. N. (2009) 'Peri-urban forests and wood energy: what are the perspectives for central Africa' in C. de Wasseige, D. Devers, P. de Marcken, R. Eba'a Atyi, R. Nasi and P. Mayaux (eds) *The Forests of the Congo Basin: State of the forest 2008.* Luxembourg: European Union.

Marysse, S. and S. Geenen (2009) 'Win–win or unequal exchange? The case of the Sino-Congolese cooperation agreements', *Journal of Modern African Studies* 47(3): 371–96.

Marysse, S. and C. Tshimanga (2013) 'La renaissance spectaculaire du secteur minier en RDC: où va la rente minière?' in S. Marysse and J. Omasombo Tshonda (eds) *Conjoncture congolaise 2012: Politique, secteur minier et gestion des ressources naturelles en RD Congo*. Tervuren and Paris: Royal Museum for Central Africa and L'Harmattan.

Mastaki Namegabe, J. L. (2006) 'Le rôle des goulots d'étranglement de la commercialisation dans l'adoption des innovations agricoles chez le producteurs vivriers du Sud-Kivu (Est de la R.D.Congo)'. Unpublished doctoral thesis, Faculté Universitaire des Sciences Agronomiques de Gembloux.

Matondi, P. B., K. Havnevik and A. Beyene (2011) 'Conclusion: land grabbing, smallholder farmers and the meaning of agro-investor-driven agrarian change in Africa' in P. B. Matondi, K. Havnevik and A. Beyene, *Biofuels, Land Grabbing and Food Security in Africa*. Uppsala and London: Nordic Africa Institute and Zed Books.

Mazalto, M. (2009) 'RD Congo: de la réforme du secteur minier à celle de l'état' in T. Trefon (ed.) *Réforme au Congo: Attentes et désillusions*. Tervuren and Paris: Les Cahiers de l'Institut Africain and L'Harmattan.

Mbalanda Kisoka, P., D. Bukayafwa Zikudieka and D. Mpotit Ilanga (eds) (n.d.) *Eau et assainissement en République Démocratique du Congo*, vol. I. Kinshasa: Avocats Verts.

Megevand, C. with A. Mosnier, J. Hourticq, K. Sanders, N. Doetinchem and C. Streck (2013) *Deforestation Trends in the Congo Basin: Reconciling economic growth and forest protection*. Washington, DC: World Bank.

Micha, J.-C. (2013) 'Fish farming in the Congo Basin, past, present and future'. Paper presented at the International Conference on Nutrition and Food Production in the Congo Basin, Royal Academy for Overseas Sciences, Brussels.

Michel, T. (2006) *Congo River*. Brussels: Luc Pire.

Misser, F. (2012) 'L'Angola, protecteur encombrant et partenaire d'avenir' in S. Marysse and J. Omasombo Tshonda (eds) *Conjoncture congolaise: Chroniques et analyses de la RD Congo en 2011*. Tervuren and Paris: Royal Museum for Central Africa and L'Harmattan.

— (2013a) 'Les aires protégées en République Démocratique du Congo: menaces et défis. L'action de l'Union européenne', *Parcs et Réserves* 68(3): 4–49.

— (2013b) *La saga d'Inga: L'histoire des barrages du fleuve Congo*. Tervuren and Paris: Royal Museum for Central Africa and L'Harmattan.

— (2013c) 'Enjeux de défis d'une province pétrolière en devenir' in S. Marysse and J. Omasombo Tshonda (eds) *Conjoncture congolaise 2012: Politique, secteur minier et gestion des ressources naturelles en RD Congo*. Tervuren and Paris: Royal Museum for Central Africa and L'Harmattan.

— (2014) 'NGOs and US Congress shun DR Congo's Inga scheme, threatening big hydropower projects', *African Energy* 272: 1–4.

Mokili Danga Kassa, J. (1998) *Politiques agricoles et promotion rurale au Congo-Zaïre 1885–1997*. Paris: L'Harmattan.

Mouzon, J.-L. (2012) 'Etude de faisabilité pour l'amélioration de l'alimentation en eau potable et de l'assainissement sur le plateau de l'Université de Kinshasa/ RD Congo'. Unpublished report. Kinshasa: ERAIFT.

Mpoyi, A. (2012) 'The importance of a legal framework for REDD+ in the Democratic Republic of Congo: proposals for legislative reform'. London: Globe International and World Summit of Legislators.

Mupepele Monti, L. (2012) L'industrie minérale Congolaise: Chiffres et défis, vol. I. Paris: L'Harmattan.

National Research Council (2008) 'Minerals, critical minerals and the U.S. economy', Washington, DC: National Academies Press.

Ndaywel è Nziem, I. (1998) Histoire générale du Congo: De l'héritage ancien à la république démocratique. Paris and Brussels: De Boeck and Larcier.

Ndikumana, L. and J. K. Boyce (1998) 'Congo's odious debt: external borrowing and capital flight in Zaire', Development and Change 29(2): 195–217.

Nest, M. (2011) Coltan. New York: Polity.

Ntoto, R. and M. F. Lunze (2013) 'Les politiques agricoles et importations alimentaires en RDC: analyse d'impact des politiques mises en œuvre'. Unpublished report. Kinshasa: Faculté des Sciences Agronomiques, University of Kinshasa.

Oxfam (2001) 'Aucune perspective en vue: la tragédie humaine du conflit en République Démocratique du Congo'. Unpublished report, Kinshasa.

Petit, P. and G. Mulumbwa Mutambwa (2005) '"La crise": lexicon and ethos of the second economy in Lubumbashi', Africa 75(4): 467–87.

Pilipili Mawezi, J. (2010) Le pétrole de la République Démocratique du Congo, Johannesburg: Southern Africa Resource Watch.

Poulton, C. (2012) 'Democratisation and the political economy of agricultural policy in Africa'. Future Agricultures working paper 043. Brighton: University of Sussex.

Prunier, G. (2009) From Genocide to Continental War: The 'Congolese' conflict and crisis of contemporary Africa. London: Hurst.

PwC with NORAD and UNDP (2012) Implementing REDD+ in the Democratic Republic of Congo: How to manage the risk of corruption. Kinshasa: PricewaterhouseCoopers (PwC), Norwegian Agency for Development Cooperation (NORAD) and United Nations Development Program (UNDP). Available at www.redd-monitor. org/2013/01/23/norway-redd-and-corruption-in-dr-congo-risks-of-corruption-will-threaten-the-implementation-of-redd-in-drc/.

Rackley, E. B. (2006) 'Democratic Republic of the Congo: undoing government by predation', Disasters 30(4): 417–23.

Reed, D. (ed.) (2015) In Pursuit of Prosperity: US foreign policy in the era of natural resource scarcity. New York: Routledge.

Reed, D. with B. Nordstrom and P. Stedman-Edwards (2015) 'Changing landscapes' in D. Reed (ed.) In Pursuit of Prosperity: US foreign policy in the era of natural resource scarcity. New York: Routledge.

Renton, D., D. Seddon and L. Zelig (2007) *The Congo: Plunder and resistance*. London: Zed Books.

République Démocratique du Congo (2012) 'Avant-projet de loi portant code de l'eau'. Kinshasa: Comité National d'Action de l'Eau et de l'Assainissement.

— (2013a) 'Fonds national REDD+: plan d'investissement (2013–2016)'. Unpublished report, Kinshasa.

— (2013b) 'Mission d'appui au Ministère de l'agriculture et du développement rural'. Unpublished report, Kinshasa.

République Démocratique du Congo and Assemblée Nationale (2005) 'Rapport de la commission spéciale chargée de l'examen de la validité des conventions à caractère économique et financier conclues pendant les guerres de 1996–1997 et de 1998'. Unpublished report, Kinshasa.

République Démocratique du Congo and Ministère des Infrastructures, Travaux Publics et Reconstruction (2007) 'Protocole d'accord'. Unpublished China–Congo agreement, Kinshasa.

République Démocratique du Congo and Ministère des Ressources Hydrauliques et Électricité (2014) 'Atlas des énergies renouvelables de la RDC'. Unpublished report, Kinshasa.

République du Zaïre (1987) 'Plan directeur du développement de la pêche'. Unpublished report, Kinshasa.

Resource Extraction Monitoring (2011) 'Note de briefing: analyse de la fiscalité forestière'. Kinshasa: Resource Extraction Monitoring.

— (2013) 'Mise en application de la loi forestière et de la gouvernance: analyse de la législation forestière de la RDC'. Cambridge: Resource Extraction Monitoring.

Ribot, J. and A. M. Larson (2012) 'Reducing REDD risks: affirmative policy on an uneven playing field', *International Journal of the Commons* 6(2): 233–54.

Roberts, A. (2006) *The Wonga Coup: Guns, thugs, and a ruthless determination to create mayhem in an oil-rich corner of Africa*. New York: Public Affairs.

Roberts, A. F. (1979) '"The ransom of ill-starred Zaire": plunder, politics, and poverty in the OTRAG concession' in G. Gran (ed.) *Zaire: The political economy of underdevelopment*. New York: Praeger.

Roxburgh, C., N. Dörr, A. Leke, A. Tazi-Riffi, A. van Wamelen, S. Lund, M. Chironga, T. Alatovik, C. Atkins, N. Terfous and T. Zeino-Mahmalat (2010) *Lions on the Move: The progress and potential of African economies*. New York: McKinsey & Company.

Rubbers, B. (2010) 'Claiming workers' rights in the Democratic Republic of Congo: the case of the *Collectif des ex-agents de la Gécamines*', *Review of African Political Economy* 37(125): 329–44.

— (2013) *Le paternalisme en question. Les anciens ouvriers de la Gécamines face à la libéralisation du secteur minier katangais (RD Congo)*. Tervuren and Paris: Les Cahiers de l'Institut Africain and L'Harmattan.

Russell, D., P. Mbile and N. Tchamou (2011) 'Farm and forest in central Africa: toward an integrated rural development strategy', *Journal of Sustainable Forestry* 30(1/2): 111–32.

Sassen, S. (2013) 'Land grabs today: feeding the disassembling of national territory', *Globalizations* 10(1): 25–46.

Schure, J., V. Ingram, S. Assembe-Mvondo, E. Mvula-Mampasi, J. Inzamba and P. Levang (2013) 'La filière bois-énergie des villes de Kinshasa et Kisangani (RDC)' in J.-N. Marien, E. Dubiez, D. Louppe and A. Larzillière (eds) *Quand la ville mange la forêt: Les défis du bois-énergies en Afrique centrale.* Versailles: Éditions Quae.

Shambaugh, J., J. Oglethorpe and R. Ham with S. Tognette (2001) *The Trampled Grass: Mitigating the impacts of armed conflict on the environment.* Washington, DC: Biodiversity Support Program.

Slade, R. (1961) *The Belgian Congo.* London: Oxford University Press.

Smith, J. H. (2011) 'Tantalus in the digital age: coltan ore, temporal dispossession, and "movement" in the eastern Democratic Republic of the Congo', *American Ethnologist* 38(1): 17–35.

SOFRECO (2012) 'Formulation/élaboration du document cadre des politiques du secteur des pêches en République Démocratique du Congo'. Unpublished report, ACP Fish II Programme, European Commission.

St-Pierre, S., P. Lorillou, T.-J. Nzakimuena, A. Rousselin and Y. Bossé (2013) 'The phased hydroelectric development approach of Inga site through adaptable and attractive steps (Democratic Republic of the Congo – DRC)'. Unpublished paper presented at Hydro-Africa international conference, Addis Ababa, Ethiopia.

Stanley, H. M. (1878) *Through the Darkest Continent or the Sources of the Nile around the Great Lakes of Equatorial Africa and down the Livingstone River to the Atlantic Ocean.* New York: Harper and Brothers.

Stengers, J. (1982) 'Le Katanga et le mirage de l'or' in J. Vansina, C. H. Perrot and R. Austen (eds) *Etudes africaines offertes à Henri Brunschwig.* Paris: École des Hautes Etudes en Sciences Sociales.

Stern, N. (2006) *Stern Review: The economics of climate change.* London: HM Treasury.

Sustainable Energy for All, République Démocratique du Congo and Programme des Nations Unies pour le Développment (2013) 'Rapport national: "Energie durable pour tous à l'horizon 2030". Programme national et stratégie'. Kinshasa: Sustainable Energy for All, République Démocratique du Congo and Programme des Nations Unies pour le Développment. Available at www.cd.undp.org/content/dam/dem_rep_congo/docs/eenv/UNDP-CD-RAPPORT-ENERGIE-DURBALE-POUR-TOUS-HORIZON-2030.pdf.

Taylor, I. (2014) 'Emerging powers, state capitalism and the oil sector in Africa', *Review of African Political Economy* 41(141): 341–57.

Tollens, E. (2004a) 'Les défis: sécurité alimentaire et cultures de rente pour l'exportation, principales orientations et avantages comparatifs de l'agriculture en R.D. Congo'. Unpublished report, Leuven.

— (2004b) 'Food security in Kinshasa: coping with adversity' in T. Trefon (ed.) *Reinventing Order in the Congo: How people respond to state failure in Kinshasa.* London: Zed Books.

Trapido, J. (2015) 'Africa's leaky giant', *New Left Review* 92 (March/April): 5–40.

Trefon, T. (ed.) (2004) *Reinventing Order in the Congo: How people respond to state failure in Kinshasa.* London: Zed Books.

— (2006) 'Industrial logging in the Democratic Republic of Congo: is a stakeholder approach possible?', *South African Journal of International Affairs* 13(2): 101–14.

— (2011a) *Congo Masquerade: The political culture of aid inefficiency and reform failure.* London: Zed Books.

— (2011b) 'Urban–rural straddling: conceptualizing the peri-urban in central Africa', *Journal of Developing Societies* 27(3/4): 421–43.

— (2013) 'Uncertainty and powerlessness in Congo 2012', *Review of African Political Economy* 40(135): 141–51.

Trefon, T. and S. Cogels (2006) 'Remote control research in central Africa', *Civilisations* 54(1/2): 145–54.

Trefon, T. and N. Kabuyaya (2009) 'Evaluation socio-économique au Parc National de la Salonga: rapport d'enquête rapide des réalisations faite par WWF et présentation de l'outil méthodologique'. Unpublished report. Kinshasa: Delegation of the European Commission.

Trefon, T. with B. Ngoy (2007) *Parcours administratifs dans un Etat en faillite: Récits de Lubumbashi (RDC).* Tervuren and Paris: L'Institut Africain and L'Harmattan.

Trefon, T., T. Hendriks, N. Kabuyaya and B. Ngoy (2010) 'L'économie politique de la filière du charbon de bois à Kinshasa et à Lubumbashi'. Working paper 2010/03. Antwerp: University of Antwerp.

Tsakala Munikengi, T. and W. Bongo-Pasi Moke Sangol (2004) 'The diploma paradox: University of Kinshasa between crisis and salvation' in T. Trefon (ed.) *Reinventing Order in the Congo: How people respond to state failure in Kinshasa.* London: Zed Books.

Tullow Oil (2013) *2013 Annual Report and Accounts.* London: Tullow Oil plc.

Turner, T. (2013) *Congo.* Cambridge and Malden, MA: Polity Press.

UN Panel of Inquiry (2003) *Report of the Panel of Experts on the Illegal Exploitation of Natural Resources and Other Forms of Wealth of the Democratic Republic of the Congo.* New York: United Nations (UN).

— (2009) *Final Report of the Panel of Experts on the Illegal Exploitation of Natural Resources and Other Forms of Wealth of the Democratic Republic of the Congo.* New York: United Nations (UN).

UNDP (2013) *Human Development Report 2013. The Rise of the South: Human progress in a diverse world.* New York: United Nations Development Programme (UNDP).

UNEP (2011a) *Water Issues in the Democratic Republic of the Congo: Challenges and opportunities.* Nairobi: United Nations Environment Programme (UNEP).

— (2011b) *The Democratic Republic of the Congo: Post-conflict environment assessment synthesis for policy makers.* Nairobi: United Nations Environment Programme (UNEP).

USAID (2010) 'USAID country profile. Property rights and resource governance: Democratic Republic of Congo'. Washington, DC: United States Agency for International Development (USAID). Available at http://usaidlandtenure. net/sites/default/files/country-profiles/full-reports/USAID_Land_Tenure_ Democratic_Republic_of_Congo_Profile_0.pdf.

van Beck, W. (2011) 'Cultural models of power in Africa' in J. Abbink and M. de Bruijn (eds) *Land, Law and Politics in Africa: Mediating conflict and reshaping the state.* Leiden: Brill.

Van Hoof, F. (2011) *Changer l'agriculture congolaise en faveur des familles paysannes: Des dynamiques paysannes dans les différentes provinces de la RDC.* Leuven: Alliance AgriCongo.

Vansina, J. (1990) *Paths in the Rainforest: Towards a history of political tradition in equatorial Africa.* Madison: University of Wisconsin Press.

Vermeulen, C. (2014) 'Enjeux autour des forêts congolaises' in S. Marysse and J. Omasombo Tshonda (eds) *Conjonctures congolaises 2013: Percée sécuritaire, flottements politiques et essor économique.* Tervuren and Paris: Royal Museum for Central Africa and L'Harmattan.

Vlassenroot, K. and T. Raeymaekers (2008) 'New political orders in the DR Congo? The transformation of regulation', *Afrika Focus* 21(2): 39–52.

Wilkie, D. S., G. Sidle, G. C. Boundzanga, S. Blake and P. Auzel (1998) 'Defaunation or deforestation: commercial logging and market hunting in northern Congo' in A. Grajal, J. C. Robinson and A. Vedder (eds) *The Impacts of Commercial Logging on Wildlife in Tropical Forests.* New Haven: Yale University Press.

Willame, J.-C. (1986) *Zaïre, l'épopée d'Inga: Chronique d'une prédation industrielle.* Paris: L'Harmattan.

World Bank (1992) 'Strategy for African mining'. Technical paper 181. Washington, DC: World Bank.

— (2008) 'Democratic Republic of Congo: growth with governance in the mining sector'. Washington, DC: World Bank.

— (2010) 'Project appraisal document on a proposed grant in the amount of SDR 33.1 million (US$50 million equivalent) to the Democratic Republic of Congo for a growth with governance in the mineral sector technical assistance project'. Washington, DC: World Bank.

World Vision (2013) *Child Miners Speak: Key findings on children and artisanal mining in Kambove DRC.* Kinshasa: World Vision.

Wunder, S. (2005) *Payments for Environmental Services: Some nuts and bolts.* CIFOR Occasional Paper 42. Bogor (Indonesia): Center for International Forestry Research (CIFOR).

WWF and Dalberg (2013) *The Economic Value of Virunga National Park*. Gland (Switzerland): WWF International.

Yates, D. (2012) *The Scramble for African Oil: Oppression, corruption and war for control of Africa's natural resources*. London: Pluto Press.

Young, C. (2012) *The Postcolonial State in Africa: Fifty years of independence, 1960–2010*. Madison: University of Wisconsin Press.

Young, C. and T. Turner (1985) *The Rise and Decline of the Zairian State*. Madison: University of Wisconsin Press.

Zaragosa Montejano, A. (2013) *In Search of Clean Water: Human rights and the mining industry in Katanga, DRC*. Antwerp: International Peace Information Service (IPIS).

Zhou, L., Y. Tian, R. B. Myneni, P. Ciais, S. Saatchi, Y. Y. Liu, S. Piao, H. Chen, E. F. Vermote, C. Song and T. Hwang (2014) 'Widespread decline of Congo rainforest greenness in the past decade', *Nature* 509: 86–90.

INDEX